NUCLEAR MATERIALS AND DISASTER RESEARCH

PROLIFERATION SECURITY MEASURES

NUCLEAR MATERIALS AND DISASTER RESEARCH

Additional books in this series can be found on Nova's website under the Series tab.

Additional E-books in this series can be found on Nova's website under the E-book tab.

DEFENSE, SECURITY AND STRATEGIES

Additional books in this series can be found on Nova's website under the Series tab.

Additional E-books in this series can be found on Nova's website under the E-book tab.

NUCLEAR MATERIALS AND DISASTER RESEARCH

PROLIFERATION SECURITY MEASURES

RODRICK D. COOKE
AND
EFREN M. VELAZQUEZ
EDITORS

Nova Science Publishers, Inc.
New York

Copyright © 2012 by Nova Science Publishers, Inc.

All rights reserved. No part of this book may be reproduced, stored in a retrieval system or transmitted in any form or by any means: electronic, electrostatic, magnetic, tape, mechanical photocopying, recording or otherwise without the written permission of the Publisher.

For permission to use material from this book please contact us:
Telephone 631-231-7269; Fax 631-231-8175
Web Site: http://www.novapublishers.com

NOTICE TO THE READER

The Publisher has taken reasonable care in the preparation of this book, but makes no expressed or implied warranty of any kind and assumes no responsibility for any errors or omissions. No liability is assumed for incidental or consequential damages in connection with or arising out of information contained in this book. The Publisher shall not be liable for any special, consequential, or exemplary damages resulting, in whole or in part, from the readers' use of, or reliance upon, this material. Any parts of this book based on government reports are so indicated and copyright is claimed for those parts to the extent applicable to compilations of such works.

Independent verification should be sought for any data, advice or recommendations contained in this book. In addition, no responsibility is assumed by the publisher for any injury and/or damage to persons or property arising from any methods, products, instructions, ideas or otherwise contained in this publication.

This publication is designed to provide accurate and authoritative information with regard to the subject matter covered herein. It is sold with the clear understanding that the Publisher is not engaged in rendering legal or any other professional services. If legal or any other expert assistance is required, the services of a competent person should be sought. FROM A DECLARATION OF PARTICIPANTS JOINTLY ADOPTED BY A COMMITTEE OF THE AMERICAN BAR ASSOCIATION AND A COMMITTEE OF PUBLISHERS.

Additional color graphics may be available in the e-book version of this book.

Library of Congress Cataloging-in-Publication Data

ISBN 978-1-62081-014-9

Published by Nova Science Publishers, Inc. † New York

CONTENTS

Preface		vii
Chapter 1	Proliferation Control Regimes: Background and Status *Mary Beth Nikitin, Paul K. Kerr and Steven A. Hildreth*	1
Chapter 2	Nuclear, Biological, Chemical, and Missile Proliferation Sanctions: Selected Current Law *Dianne E. Rennack*	63
Chapter 3	Proliferation Security Initiative (PSI) *Mary Beth Nikitin*	119
Index		135

PREFACE

Weapons of mass destruction (WMD), especially in the hands of radical states and terrorists, represent a major threat to U.S. national security interests. Multilateral regimes were established to restrict trade in nuclear, chemical, and biological weapons and missile technologies, and to monitor their civil applications. Congress may consider the efficacy of these regimes in considering the potential renewal of the Export Administration Act, as well as other proliferation-specific legislation in the 111th Congress. This book provides background and current status information on nuclear nonproliferation regimes which encompass several treaties, extensive multilateral and bilateral diplomatic agreements, multilateral organizations and domestic agencies, and the domestic laws of participating countries.

Chapter 1- Weapons of mass destruction (WMD), especially in the hands of radical states and terrorists, represent a major threat to U.S. national security interests. Multilateral regimes were established to restrict trade in nuclear, chemical, and biological weapons and missile technologies, and to monitor their civil applications. Congress may consider the efficacy of these regimes in considering the potential renewal of the Export Administration Act, as well as other proliferation-specific legislation in the 111th Congress. This report provides background and current status information on the regimes.

The nuclear nonproliferation regime encompasses several treaties, extensive multilateral and bilateral diplomatic agreements, multilateral organizations and domestic agencies, and the domestic laws of participating countries. Since the dawn of the nuclear age, U.S. leadership has been crucial in developing the regime. While there is almost universal international agreement opposing the further spread of nuclear weapons, several challenges to the regime have arisen in recent years: India and Pakistan tested nuclear weapons in 1998, North Korea withdrew from the Nuclear Nonproliferation Treaty (NPT) in 2003 and tested a nuclear explosive device in 2006 and 2009, Libya gave up a clandestine nuclear weapons program in 2004, and Iran was found to be in non-compliance with its treaty obligations in 2005. The discovery of the nuclear black market network run by A.Q. Khan spurred new thinking about how to strengthen the regime, including greater restrictions on sensitive technology. However, the extension of civil nuclear cooperation by the United States and other countries to India, a non-party to the NPT with nuclear weapons, has raised questions about what benefits still exist for non-nuclear-weapons states that remain in the treaty regime.

Chapter 2- The proliferation of nuclear, biological, and chemical weapons, and the means to deliver them, are front and center today for policy makers who guide and form U.S. foreign policy and national security policy, and economic sanctions are considered a valuable asset in the national security and foreign policy toolbox. The United States currently maintains robust sanctions regimes against foreign governments it has identified as proliferators (particularly Iran, North Korea, and Syria). If the 112th Congress takes up even a fraction of the proposals introduced by its predecessor involving economic sanctions, the president and the Departments of State, Commerce, and Treasury—those agencies that implement and administer the bulk of sanctions regimes—will likely find the role of Congress in determining the use of sanctions also robust.

This report offers a listing and brief description of legal provisions that require or authorize the imposition of some form of economic sanction against countries, companies, persons, or entities that violate U.S. nonproliferation norms. For each provision, information is included on what triggers the imposition of sanctions, their duration, what authority the president has to delay or abstain from imposing sanctions, and what authority the president has to waive the imposition of sanctions.

Chapter 3- The Proliferation Security Initiative (PSI) was formed to increase international cooperation in interdicting shipments of weapons of mass destruction (WMD), their delivery systems, and related materials. The Initiative was announced by President Bush on May 31, 2003. PSI does not create a new legal framework but aims to use existing national authorities and international law to achieve its goals. Initially, 11 nations signed on to the "Statement of Interdiction Principles" that guides PSI cooperation. As of January 2011, 97 countries (plus the Holy See) have committed formally to the PSI principles, although the extent of participation may vary by country. PSI has no secretariat, but an Operational Experts Group (OEG), made up of 21 PSI participants, coordinates activities.

Although WMD interdiction efforts took place with international cooperation before PSI was formed, supporters argue that PSI training exercises and boarding agreements give a structure and expectation of cooperation that will improve interdiction efforts. Many observers believe that PSI's "strengthened political commitment of like-minded states" to cooperate on interdiction is a successful approach to counter-proliferation policy. But some caution that it may be difficult to measure the initiative's effectiveness, guarantee even participation, or sustain the effort over time in the absence of a formal multilateral framework. Others support expanding membership and improving inter-governmental and U.S. interagency coordination as the best way to improve the program. President Obama in an April 2009 speech said that PSI should be turned into a "durable international institution." The administration's 2010 Nuclear Security Strategy said it would work to turn PSI into a "durable international effort." The 2010 Nuclear Posture Review included PSI as a key part of the policy to impede sensitive nuclear trade.

In: Proliferation Security Measures
Editors: R. Cooke & E. Velazquez

ISBN: 978-1-62081-014-9
© 2012 Nova Science Publishers, Inc

Chapter 1

PROLIFERATION CONTROL REGIMES: BACKGROUND AND STATUS[*]

Mary Beth Nikitin, Paul K. Kerr and Steven A. Hildreth

SUMMARY

Weapons of mass destruction (WMD), especially in the hands of radical states and terrorists, represent a major threat to U.S. national security interests. Multilateral regimes were established to restrict trade in nuclear, chemical, and biological weapons and missile technologies, and to monitor their civil applications. Congress may consider the efficacy of these regimes in considering the potential renewal of the Export Administration Act, as well as other proliferation-specific legislation in the 111th Congress. This report provides background and current status information on the regimes.

The nuclear nonproliferation regime encompasses several treaties, extensive multilateral and bilateral diplomatic agreements, multilateral organizations and domestic agencies, and the domestic laws of participating countries. Since the dawn of the nuclear age, U.S. leadership has been crucial in developing the regime. While there is almost universal

---

[*] This is an edited, reformatted and augmented version of a Congressional Research Service publication, CRS Report for Congress RL31559, prepared for Members and Committees of Congress, from www.crs.gov, dated October 18, 2010.

international agreement opposing the further spread of nuclear weapons, several challenges to the regime have arisen in recent years: India and Pakistan tested nuclear weapons in 1998, North Korea withdrew from the Nuclear Nonproliferation Treaty (NPT) in 2003 and tested a nuclear explosive device in 2006 and 2009, Libya gave up a clandestine nuclear weapons program in 2004, and Iran was found to be in non-compliance with its treaty obligations in 2005. The discovery of the nuclear black market network run by A.Q. Khan spurred new thinking about how to strengthen the regime, including greater restrictions on sensitive technology. However, the extension of civil nuclear cooperation by the United States and other countries to India, a non-party to the NPT with nuclear weapons, has raised questions about what benefits still exist for non-nuclear-weapons states that remain in the treaty regime.

The chemical and biological weapons (CBW) nonproliferation regimes contain three elements: the Chemical Weapons Convention (CWC), the Biological and Toxin Weapons Convention (BWC), and the Australia Group. The informal Australia Group coordinates export controls on CBW-related materials and technology. After 25 years of negotiations, the CWC entered into force in April 1997. It prohibits the development, production, stockpiling, transfer, and use of chemical weapons, and mandates the destruction of existing chemical weapon arsenals. Since its 1972 inception, BWC state parties have failed to agree on a verification mechanism.

The missile nonproliferation regime is founded not on a treaty, but an informal agreement created in 1987, the Missile Technology Control Regime (MTCR). The MTCR's goal is to limit the spread of missiles capable of carrying nuclear weapons. Thirty-four countries now adhere to the guidelines, which have been modified over time to include missile systems designed for the delivery of chemical and biological weapons. The regime, which has no enforcement organization, is thought to have been instrumental in blocking several missile programs, but it has been unable to stop North Korean missile development, production, and exports, or to win the full cooperation of Russian and Chinese entities.

INTRODUCTION

The United States has historically led the international community in establishing regimes intended to limit the spread of nuclear, chemical, and biological weapons and missiles. The regimes and their member countries use cooperative and coercive measures to achieve nonproliferation and counterproliferation objectives.

Multilateral agreements and organizations are supplemented by strong bilateral cooperation among key allies, unilateral political and economic

Proliferation Control Regimes: Background and Status   3

actions, and recourse to military operations should they become necessary. Congress supports the nonproliferation regimes primarily by providing statutory authority and funding for U.S. participation, establishing policy, and mandating punitive actions to help enforce the international standards set by the regimes.

The term "regime" often refers to the entire array of international agreements, multilateral organizations, national laws, regulations, and policies to prevent the spread of dangerous weapons and technologies. The nuclear nonproliferation regime is presently the most extensive, followed by those dealing with chemical and biological weapons, and then by the missile regime. The difficulty of producing nuclear weapons material (highly enriched uranium or plutonium) and the great awareness of nuclear weapons' destructiveness together have been conducive to creating a complex regime with widespread agreement on the priority of nuclear nonproliferation. Chemical weapons are easier to make and rely on readily available precursors, and they are far less destructive.

Biological weapons also rely on dual-use technology, and as technology has spread, efforts to build a more extensive control regime have intensified. Finally, there is no international consensus on the danger of missile proliferation to support a nonproliferation treaty or a binding regime with enforcement mechanisms.

A key aspect of all the regimes is their attempt to control exports of sensitive goods and technologies through supplier agreements. These are the Nuclear Suppliers Group and the Zangger Committee for nuclear technology, the Australia Group for chemical and biological weapons technology, and the Missile Technology Control Regime. In the last decade, these export control regimes have expanded their membership, expanded and refined their control lists, and increased coordination among member states. At the same time, however, the non-binding nature of some of the regimes and growing resistance to them by certain countries, including some regime members, limits their effectiveness.

A major dilemma is whether to include new members, that may not be U.S. allies and may not have reliable export controls, or to limit membership to countries with excellent nonproliferation credentials. Regime members are afforded special access to controlled technology by the other members, so this issue also affects decisions on whether to include non-allies.

Table 1 lists the proliferation control regimes, their components and statutory authority. There are many arms control treaties and other activities that address aspects of WMD and conventional weapons beyond the regimes covered in this report.[1]

Status and Trends

Although proliferation control regimes are a useful tool in preventing dangerous technology transfers, several factors undermine their effectiveness. One is the difficulty of addressing underlying motivations of countries to acquire weapons of mass destruction (WMD). Regional security conditions as well as the desire to compensate for other countries' superior conventional or unconventional forces have been common motivations for WMD programs. Some countries may want WMD to dominate their adversaries. Prestige is another reason why certain countries seek WMD. Another factor working against the regimes is the steady diffusion of technology over time—much of the most significant WMD technology is 50 years old, and growing access to dual-use equipment makes it easier for countries or groups to build their own WMD production facilities from commonly available civilian equipment.

There are at least two problems common to all of the nonproliferation regimes—the lack of universal membership and gaps in verification. In the nuclear regime, India, Pakistan, North Korea, and Israel are not members of the NPT. Apart from diplomatic questions about how to treat their status as states with nuclear weapons not sanctioned by the NPT, those countries are not bound by that treaty's prohibition on sharing nuclear technology, nor are they committed to eventually eliminating these weapons. They are also not members of the export control groups. The international community struggles with how to bring these states into the nonproliferation regimes without tacitly agreeing to their acquisition of nuclear weapons. For example, a major objection to the U.S. nuclear cooperation agreement with India was the perception that it legitimizes India's nuclear weapons program without extracting any significant concessions on limiting its nuclear arsenal. Like India, Pakistan is not bound by any NPT obligations, whether or not Pakistani scientist A.Q. Khan sold nuclear technology on the black market with or without Pakistani government acquiescence. Revelations in 2004 of centrifuge enrichment technology sales to Libya, Iran, and North Korea galvanized the international community to examine strengthening implementation of national export controls and interdiction.

In the chemical and biological weapons (CBW) area, some states suspected of having military programs are still outside the treaty. Within the treaties, there are some members (e.g., Iran under the CWC and Russia under the BWC) suspected of continuing programs. In the missile area, although the Hague Code of Conduct has widespread membership, MTCR is still not adhered to by many states (e.g., China, North Korea) that are responsible for proliferating missile technologies.

Continued diplomatic support for the treaties and export control regimes may face some hurdles. In the nuclear nonproliferation regime, many non-weapons states link their continued cooperation with progress in implementing Article VI of the treaty (steps toward eventual nuclear disarmament by the five nuclear weapons states).

In recent years, several developments have generated criticism: the United States' abrogation of the Anti-Ballistic Missile (ABM) Treaty; conclusion of the Moscow Treaty, which many criticize as having little real impact and no verification; the U.S. Senate's rejection of the Comprehensive Test Ban Treaty in 1999; failure to proceed on a fissile material production cutoff treaty in Geneva; and perceived interest in new U.S. nuclear weapons. Some non-nuclear-weapon states are also resistant to accepting any limitations on nuclear technology exports involving advanced fuel production technology that has the potential to produce weapons grade material.

These states view such restrictions as limiting their access to peaceful nuclear technology as guaranteed by the NPT. Thus, as dual-use equipment in all WMD fields becomes more widespread, there may be a higher expectation that exporters will need to better control where their technology goes and how it is used.

State-to-State Relations

In addition to a formal framework of control agreements, close political relationships with key allies and other countries are very important for U.S. efforts to counter the spread and the use of WMD. Initiatives by allies, such as the G-8 Global Partnership to Combat the Spread of WMD, demonstrate resolve to tackle specific proliferation problems. In May 2003, President Bush launched the "Proliferation Security Initiative" (see description below). Many of these relationships, nonetheless, are strongly influenced by other political, military, and economic issues that sometimes take precedence over proliferation concerns. In practice, nonproliferation competes with important policy objectives such as trade, regional issues, and domestic political considerations, and uneven implementation of nonproliferation policy can result.

Table 1. Proliferation Control Regimes

Regime	Formal Treaties	Suppliers Groups and Informal Agreements	International Organization	U.S. Legal Framework	U.S. Government Agencies
Nuclear	Nuclear Nonproliferation Treaty (NPT), 1970 Convention on Physical Protection of Nuclear Material, 1987 + Amendment Treaty of Tlatelolco Treaty of Rarotonga Treaty of Pelindaba Treaty of Bangkok Treaty on a nuclear-weapons-free-zone (NWFZ) in Central Asia START Protocols Treaty of Moscow, 2002	Zangger Committee, 1971 Nuclear Suppliers Group, 1975 G-8	International Atomic Energy Agency (IAEA) U.N. Conference on Disarmament	AEA, 1954 NNPA, 1978 FAA, 1961 AECA, 1976 EAA, 1979 NPPA, 1994 Ex-Im Bank, 1945 Nunn-Lugar 1991 Iran-Iraq Arms Non-proliferation (NP) Act, 1992 Iran, Syria, No. Korea NP Act	State, Defense, Commerce, Energy (+ national laboratories), Treasury, NRC, intelligence agencies
Chemical and Biological	Geneva Protocol, 1925 Chemical Weapons Convention (CWC) 1993 Biological and Toxin Weapons Convention (BWC)	Australia Group, 1984	OPCW U.N. Conference on Disarmament	EAA, 1979 AECA, 1976 Biological Weapons Anti-Terrorism Act Chem-Bio Weapons Control Warfare Elimination Act, 1991 Nunn-Lugar Freedom Support Act Iran-Iraq Arms NP Act, 1992 Iran, Syria, No. Korea NP Act	State, Defense, Commerce, Treasury, intelligence agencies

Regime	Formal Treaties	Suppliers Groups and Informal Agreements	International Organization	U.S. Legal Framework	U.S. Government Agencies
Missiles		Missile Technology Control Regime, 1987 International Code of Conduct, 2002		FAA, 1961 AECA, 1976 EAA, 1979 Missile Tech. Control Act, 1990 Freedom Support Act Iran-Iraq NP Act Iran, Syria, No. Korea NP Act	State, Defense, Commerce, Treasury, NASA intelligence agencies

Source: Congressional Research Service.

Notes: Legislation abbreviations: AEA—Atomic Energy Act; AECA—Arms Export Control Act; EAA—Export Administration Act; FAA—Foreign Assistance Act; NNPA— Nuclear Nonproliferation Act of 1978; NPPA—Nuclear Proliferation Prevention Act.

A more difficult challenge exists when U.S. allies and friends seek WMD and missiles of their own or transfer WMD technology. Perhaps the hardest challenge for nonproliferation policies is to reduce the desire of countries for weapons of mass destruction. It is sometimes possible to change regional security conditions through alliances, conventional arms transfers, arms control, or negotiations aimed at settling conflicts. However, eliminating underlying motivations takes time, and the next best option may be to delay WMD development for as long as possible, or to attempt to impact a country's calculation of the costs of pursuing these weapons. Libya's decision in December 2003 to give up its nuclear, chemical weapons, and missile programs is a good example of a state that apparently decided the costs of WMD programs exceeded their benefits.

Unilaterally, the United States uses sanctions to support its nonproliferation objectives. Various laws authorize or require the president to impose unilateral sanctions on countries that acquire, use, or help other countries to obtain WMD or missiles. Sanctions can affect U.S. aid, cooperation, and impose restrictions on U.S. technology exports. The effectiveness of sanctions often depends on persuading other countries to support or respect U.S. sanctions. Even without multilateral support, sanctions can still highlight strong U.S. opposition to WMD proliferation. However, strong sanctions are rarely imposed on U.S. friends or allies that acquire WMD.

Counterproliferation, Intelligence, and Deterrence

U.S. armed forces have developed programs to help prevent the spread of WMD, to deter or prevent their use, and to protect against their effects. Defense cooperation and arms transfers to U.S. allies can ease concerns about security that can lead them to consider acquiring WMD, and also signal potential adversaries that acquisition or use of WMD may evoke a strong military response. U.S. conventional and nuclear military capabilities and the threat of retaliation help deter WMD attacks against U.S. forces, territory, or allies. Counterproliferation capabilities have been expanded in recent years to include more advanced "passive" and "active" defense measures. Passive counterproliferation tools include protective gear such as gas masks and detectors to warn of the presence of WMD. Active measures include missile defenses to protect U.S. territory, forces, and allies; precision-guided penetrating munitions and special operation forces to attack WMD installations; and intelligence gathering and processing capabilities. Intelligence is crucial to U.S. nonproliferation efforts, particularly in helping shape policy options. Intelligence agencies track foreign WMD programs, monitor treaty compliance, and attempt to detect transfers of WMD goods and technology. The United States cooperates with certain allies to prepare for possible counterproliferation actions. Although counterproliferation is a main pillar of U.S. strategy to combat WMD, political and technical hurdles (hiddenunderground bunkers, locations near civilians, etc.) tend to make counterproliferation a last resort, after other options have failed.

One key tool of counterproliferation has been interdiction of WMD-related equipment shipments at sea, on land, and by air. President Bush announced the Proliferation Security Initiative (PSI) on May 31, 2003. PSI, described as an activity rather than an organization, aims to better coordinate like-minded countries' efforts to interdict such illicit shipments, based on existing legal authorities.[2]

Congressional Role

Congress has been actively engaged in nonproliferation legislation for close to 60 years. In addition to laws affecting diplomacy, treaty implementation and military options, legislation effecting restrictions on foreign aid, sanctions, and export controls helps establish nonproliferation policy and congressional oversight of executive branch nonproliferation and counterproliferation policies.

Congress enacted strict controls on nuclear energy and cooperation in the first Atomic Energy Act of 1946. By the 1950s, however, it became clear that the U.S. nuclear weapons program needed materials from abroad and that pure denial of materials and technology had neither stopped the Soviet Union nor the UK from acquiring nuclear weapons. The 1954 revision of the Atomic Energy Act reflected a shift in strategy from that of prevention through denial to one of influence through cooperation. However, as allies planned to sell sensitive enrichment and reprocessing equipment to states outside of the NPT in the 1970s (e.g., Pakistan, South Korea, and Brazil), Congress reacted by passing several laws to slow down nuclear commerce and implement sanctions against those states clandestinely pursuing nuclear weapons. Controls on exports of chemical and biological agents with military applications and missiles have been regulated under the Arms Export Control Act (AECA) of 1968, and their dual-use technologies have been regulated under the Export

Administration Act (EAA) of 1979 and its predecessors, but these controls were implemented relatively later in the 1980s. *Table 2* lists the major U.S. laws enacted to limit the transfer of WMD and WMD technology. Over time, most laws have been amended to address the range of WMD threats, but there are a few laws that address only one kind of weapon of mass destruction; some laws have focused on a proliferation threat from a particular country. Nunn-Lugar-related legislation and the Freedom Support Act address the range of WMD, but focus on Russia and the NIS. In addition, legislation related to Iran and Syria spans the range of WMD proliferation. See *Appendix B* for relevant text from nonproliferation-related legislation.

Organization of the Report

The following sections will describe the nuclear, biological, chemical, and missile nonproliferation regimes. Each section will include (1) a background section with a brief history of the regime; (2) a section setting out the treaties and agreements that authorize or affect the regime; (3) a brief description of how the regime is implemented; (4) U.S. laws authorizing or affecting the regime; and (5) issues for 111th Congress. More detailed information on regime membership, specific provisions in law and relevant executive orders are contained in appendices.

THE NUCLEAR NONPROLIFERATION REGIME

The nuclear nonproliferation regime encompasses several treaties, extensive multilateral and bilateral diplomatic agreements, multilateral organizations and domestic agencies, and the domestic laws of participating countries. Since the dawn of the nuclear age, U.S. leadership has been crucial in developing the regime. While there is almost universal international agreement opposing the further spread of nuclear weapons, several challenges have arisen in recent years: India and Pakistan tested nuclear weapons in 1998; North Korea withdrew from the Nuclear Nonproliferation Treaty (NPT) in 2003 and tested a nuclear device in 2006 and 2009; Libya gave up a clandestine nuclear weapons program in 2004, and Iran was found to be in non-compliance with its treaty obligations in 2005. The discovery of the nuclear black market network run by A.Q. Khan has spurred new thinking about how to strengthen the regime, including enhanced export controls and greater restrictions on sensitive technology.

Table 2. U.S. Legal Framework for Proliferation Control

Title	Public Law	Application	Nuclear	Chemical	Biological	Missiles	Target Country	Notes
Export-Import Bank Act of 1945	P.L. 79-173 P.L. 107-189 reauth	financing cutoff for nuclear safeguards violations and nuclear tests after 1977	X	X	X	X	Various	P.L. 107-189 added enforcement of AECA, EAA, IEEPA as justification for denying financing, extending purview of law to CW/BW/missile areas
Atomic Energy Act 1954	P.L. 83-703	exports; cutoff in nuclear cooperation	X Sec 129				Various	P.L. 95-242 added Sec 129
Foreign Assistance Act 1961	P.L. 87-195	aid cutoff	X Sec 307e Sec 620 E (e) Sec 620 (y)	X	X	X Sec 498 A(b)	Various Russia Cuba	NPPA repealed relevant sections in FAA and placed them in AECA. Reference to FAA is deemed now to refer to sections 101 or 102 in AECA.
Arms Export Control Act 1968	P.L. 90-629	exports, aid cutoff; sanctions	X Sec 3f Sec 101, 102*	X Sec 81**	X Sec 81	X Sec 72, 73, 74	Various	* NPPA 94 **P.L. 102-182 added in 1991
Nuclear Nonproliferation Act 1978	P.L. 95-242	sanctions	X				Various	See Atomic Energy Act
Export Administration Act 1979	P.L. 96-72	export controls	X Sec 5, 6	X Sec 6(m), 11C	X Sec 6(m), 11C	X Sec 5, 6(l), 11B	Various	Sec 11C added in 1991 by P.L. 102-182.

Table 2. (Continued)

Title	Public Law	Application	Nuclear	Chemical	Biological	Missiles	Target Country	Notes
Biological Anti-Terrorism Act 1989	P.L. 101-298	treaty: BWC			X		N.A.	Implements BWC
Missile Technology Control Act 1990	P.L. 101-510, Title XVII	sanctions				X	Various	Added Chapter VII to AECA, Sections 6 (L) and 11B to EAA 1979
Chemical and Biological Weapons Control and Warfare Elimination Act 1991*	P.L. 102-182, Title III	sanctions		X	X		Various	
Nunn-Lugar 1991	P.L. 102-228	assistance programs	X	X	X	X	Russia	Amendment to CFE Treaty;
Cooperative Threat Reduction Act 1993	P.L. 103-160		X	X	X	X		Title XI
Iran-Iraq Arms Nonproliferation Act 1992	P.L. 102-484 Title XVI	sanctions	X	X	X	X	Iran, Iraq	
Freedom Support Act	P.L. 102-511 Title V	assistance programs	X	X	X	X	NIS	
Nuclear Proliferation Prevention Act 1994	P.L. 103-236, Title VIII	sanctions	X				Various	Consolidated np legislation into AECA, moving it from FAA
Chemical Weapons Convention Implementation Act	P.L. 105-277	treaty: CWC		X			N.A.	

Title	Public Law	Application	Nuclear	Chemical	Biological	Missiles	Target Country	Notes
1998								
North Korea Threat Reduction Act of 1999	P.L. 106-113 (consolidated appropriations)	assistance; nuclear cooperation	X				North Korea	
Iran, North Korea and Syria Nonproliferation Act 2006	P.L. 109-112 (amended by P.L. 109-353)	third-party sanctions	X	X	X	X	Iran, North Korea, Syria	Covers transfers to and from states
Syria Accountability and Lebanese Sovereignty Restoration Act of 2003	P.L. 108-175	Export controls, sanctions	X	X	X	X	Syria	
Foreign Operations, Export Financing, and Related Programs Appropriations Act, 2006	P.L. 109-102	Financing, assistance cutoff	X				Russia	
Iran & Libya Sanctions Act	P.L. 109-267 (amended by H.R. 5877)	third-party sanctions	X	X	X	X	Iran, Libya	Renewed by H.R. 6198, Iran Freedom Support Act until 2011, signed by president on Sept. 30, 2006

However, the extension of civil nuclear cooperation by the United States and other countries to India, a non-party to the NPT, has raised questions about what benefits still exist for non-nuclear-weapons states that remain within the treaty regime.

In 2009, there were five declared nuclear weapons states (United States, Russia, Great Britain, France, China), three *de facto* nuclear weapons states (India, Israel, Pakistan), and one country— North Korea—that has probably produced enough plutonium for at least half a dozen nuclear bombs and has tested two nuclear devices.[3] This is considerably less than predicted 40 years ago, when President Kennedy warned of the possibility that, by the 1970s, the United States could "face a world in which fifteen or twenty or twenty-five nations may have these weapons."

The nonproliferation regime has not stopped all proliferation, but it has helped restrain nuclear ambitions and solidified an international norm of behavior strongly condemning proliferation. Many countries that could make nuclear weapons have not, but some have at one time or another taken significant steps towards acquiring a nuclear weapons capability. Argentina, Brazil, South Africa, Iran, Iraq, North Korea, Taiwan, Sweden, and South Korea all have had nuclear weapons development programs. Both Japan and Germany had nuclear weapons programs during the Second World War, but did not succeed in making nuclear weapons before their programs were halted at the end of the war. Argentina, Brazil, South Korea, Sweden, Taiwan, and South Africa abandoned their nuclear weapons programs and joined the NPT as non-nuclear-weapons states. South Africa was the only country in this group to have built and abandoned actual warheads.[4] Ukraine, Kazakhstan, and Belarus inherited nuclear weapons on their soil when the Soviet Union collapsed, but opted to join the NPT as non-nuclear-weapons states (the warheads were returned to Russia). Despite its membership as a non-nuclear-weapons state in the NPT, Libya gave up a clandestine nuclear weapons program in December 2003.[5]

While only a few countries maintain an interest in developing nuclear weapons, it is difficult to predict how many countries or terrorist groups may in the future want a nuclear weapons capability. Some of the major challenges in preventing nuclear proliferation will include the following:

- controlling access to sensitive nuclear fuel cycle technologies, such as uranium enrichment and spent fuel reprocessing, via multilateral ownership or some other mechanism;

Proliferation Control Regimes: Background and Status

- strengthening physical protection of all source and special nuclear materials globally, with continued emphasis on controlling nuclear materials smuggling from the former Soviet Union and other countries with weak controls;
- strengthening the International Atomic Energy Agency's safeguards system;
- strengthening national export control laws and regulations, per U.N. Security Council Resolution 1540;
- negotiating with North Korea to verify and dismantle its nuclear weapons program;
- restraining nuclear proliferation in India and Pakistan;
- restraining nuclear programs in the Middle East, including those of Israel and Iran;
- preventing U.S. technology from aiding the development of WMD and delivery systems in foreign countries;
- strengthening international verification and enforcement of nonproliferation agreements.

Treaties and Agreements

The NPT is the centerpiece of nuclear nonproliferation efforts. Other relevant treaties include regional nuclear-weapon-free zones and the Convention on the Physical Protection of Nuclear Material. In addition to these multilateral treaties, the United States has also entered into bilateral agreements and multilateral initiatives, such as the G-8 Global Partnership to Combat WMD. Finally, actions the United States takes in related areas of arms control may have an impact on the nonproliferation regime.

Treaty on the Nonproliferation of Nuclear Weapons (NPT), 1970

It took just three months after the bombing of Hiroshima and Nagasaki in 1945 for the first proposals to emerge from governments to control the "destructive uses" of nuclear energy. It took 25 years, however, for the NPT to emerge as the blueprint for nuclear nonproliferation.[6] In 1968, the treaty demarcated nuclear-weapon states from non-nuclear-weapon states by defining nuclear-weapon states as those states that have manufactured and exploded a nuclear weapon or othernuclear explosive device prior to January 1, 1967. This definition implied that there would only ever be five "legitimate" nuclear-weapon states—the United States, Russia, Great Britain, France, and China. All other states would join as non-nuclear-weapon states, agreeing not to acquire nuclear weapons in exchange for assistance in the peaceful uses of nuclear energy. As of January 2010, there are 189 parties to the NPT, including all five nuclear weapons states.[7] Only four countries are not members of the treaty. North Korea withdrew from the treaty officially in April 2003. India, Israel, and Pakistan have never been members of the treaty.

The pledge not to acquire nuclear weapons is verified through the application of "nuclear safeguards" measures. The International Atomic Energy Agency (IAEA), founded in 1957, devised a system of nuclear material accountancy coupled with periodic and special inspections to ensure that nuclear material is not diverted from peaceful uses to military uses. Each nonnuclear-weapon-state party to the NPT must negotiate an agreement with the IAEA to submit all nuclear material in its possession to regular inspections.[8] After learning several lessons from Iraq's and North Korea's clandestine nuclear programs, the IAEA launched a major effort to strengthen its safeguards system (see below) in 1992.

The incentive for non-nuclear-weapon states to submit to inspections is a promise by advanced nuclear countries to promote "the fullest possible exchange of equipment, materials and scientific and technological information for the peaceful uses of nuclear energy."[9] For their part, the nuclear-weapon states agree to "pursue negotiations in good faith on effective measures relating to cessation of the nuclear arms race at an early date and to nuclear disarmament."[10]

In 1995, NPT members voted to make the treaty permanent. The members also agreed on a stronger review process to oversee compliance with the treaty. However, many members of the NPT are dissatisfied, particularly with perceived lack of progress on nuclear disarmament, and the future of the treaty is not guaranteed (see discussion of implementation). Member states will discuss the status of the treaty at a Review Conference in May 2010.

Convention on the Physical Protection of Nuclear Material, 1987

The Convention on the Physical Protection of Nuclear Material[11] sets international standards for nuclear trade and commerce. The treaty had 142 parties in January 2010. The convention outlines security requirements for the protection of nuclear materials against terrorism and provides for the prosecution and punishment of offenders of international nuclear trade laws. Parties to the treaty agree to report to the IAEA on the disposition of nuclear materials being transported and agree to provide appropriate security during such transport.

For several years, the United States worked to strengthen this treaty to address nuclear terrorism by extending controls to domestic facility security, not just transportation. In July 2005, states parties convened to amend the convention. They extended the convention's scope to cover not only nuclear material in international transport, but also nuclear material in domestic use, storage, and transport, as well as the protection of nuclear material and facilities from sabotage. The new rules will come into effect once they have been ratified by two-thirds of the states parties of the convention, which could take several years. As of December 17, 2009, only 33 states had deposited their instruments of ratification, acceptance, or approval of the amendment with the depositary. On September 4, 2007, President Bush submitted the amendment to the Senate for its advice and consent on ratification. The Senate Committee on Foreign Relations recommended that the Senate give its advice and consent on September 11, 2008. The Senate must approve implementing legislation before the United States deposits its instrument of ratification to the amendment.

Related Arms Control Agreements

In the 1990s, the Comprehensive Test Ban Treaty (CTBT) was seen as the next step toward nuclear disarmament, but also a means to prevent the further spread of nuclear weapons. By the mid-1990s, all nuclear-weapons states were observing a moratorium on testing, which the treaty would make permanent. The parties completed negotiations and signed the CTBT in 1996; President Clinton submitted the treaty to the Senate in September 1997, and in 1999 the Senate voted against the treaty.[12] President Obama has said his administration will pursue U.S. CTBT ratification.

Another initiative dating from the 1990s is the effort to negotiate a treaty banning the production of fissile materials for weapons, or fissile material cut-off treaty (FMCT). Some perceive such a ban on producing fissile material for weapons as much more relevant today than it was a decade ago. Concern about terrorist access to large stockpiles of fissile material has only grown since the Cooperative Threat Reduction programs began in the early 1990s and particularly since September 11, 2001. Revelations about Pakistani scientist A.Q. Khan's nuclear black market sales of uranium enrichment technology in 2004 have spurred efforts not only to shut down networks, but restrict even "legitimate" technology transfer. Recent proposals to strengthen the nonproliferation regime, including those of Mohamed El Baradei, former director general of the International Atomic Energy Agency (IAEA), have focused on tighter controls on sensitive nuclear fuel cycle technologies, renewed disarmament effort, and creative approaches toward states outside the Nuclear Nonproliferation Treaty (NPT)—India, Pakistan, and Israel.[13] An FMCT could play a pivotal role in implementing that agenda, by helping to gain broad support for new multilateral arrangements to restrict enrichment and reprocessing, helping to strengthen consensus among NPT parties, and by achieving a concrete step toward disarmament.[14] The Obama administration said it will "lead a global effort to negotiate a verifiable treaty ending the production of fissile materials for weapons purposes."[15]

Nuclear-Weapon-Free Zones

In the last 35 years, some states have concluded treaties to declare their regions to be "nuclear weapons-free." These regions now include most of the globe—Latin America, Central and Southeast Asia, the South Pacific, Africa, and Central Asia.

Treaty for the Prohibition of Nuclear Weapons in Latin America (Treaty of Tlatelolco)

The Treaty of Tlatelolco[16] establishes a nuclear-weapon-free zone (NWFZ) in Latin America. Protocol I of the treaty obligates non-Latin American countries that have territories in the zone (United States, UK, Netherlands, France) to accept the provisions of the treaty with respect to those territories. Protocol II contains a negative security pledge by the nuclear weapons states (China, France, Russia, UK, United States) "not to use or threaten to use nuclear weapons against the Contracting Parties of the Treaty." In 1994, treaty holdouts Argentina, Brazil, and Chile signed on, and in 1995 Cuba signed the treaty (which entered into force in 2002). The Agency for the Prohibition of Nuclear Weapons in Latin America and the Caribbean (OPANAL) in Mexico City serves as Secretariat for treaty implementation.

South Pacific Nuclear Free Zone (Treaty of Rarotonga)

Thirteen nations of the South Pacific have established a NWFZ for their region which prohibits the possession of nuclear weapons by its members and bans the manufacture or permanent emplacement of nuclear weapons within the zone by signatories outside of the Pacific region. The treaty does not inhibit transit through the zone by nuclear-armed or -powered military ships or aircraft. In 1996, the United States, France, and Britain signed the protocols to the treaty, which are nearly identical to those of the Treaty of Tlatelolco.

Before signing the treaty protocols, France conducted its last nuclear tests at its test site in French Polynesia. The United States is the only nuclear-weapon state that has not ratified the protocol.

African Nuclear Weapon-Free-Zone Treaty (Treaty of Pelindaba)

In April 1996, the Treaty of Pelindaba, establishing Africa as a NWFZ, was opened for signature. The treaty now has 53 signatures and 21 ratifications. It will enter into force after the 28th ratification. The African NWFZ closely follows the models of the South Pacific and Latin American zones, and thus was able to attract the support of the United States and other weapons states after certain criteria were satisfied. This nuclear-weapon-free zone is not yet in force, and the United States and Russia have not ratified (but have signed) the relevant protocol.

Southeast Asia Nuclear Weapon-Free-Zone (Treaty of Bangkok)

A group of 10 Southeast Asian nations declared a NWFZ for their region in December 1995, and the treaty entered into force in 1997. The United States and other weapons states declined to sign the protocols to the zone because the treaty contained controversial definitions of its members' sovereignty over territorial seas.

The United States maintains that the language of the treaty is inconsistent with the Law of the Sea and could inflame territorial disputes as well as interfere with rights of passage. Modifications of the language are under consideration. In 1999, China announced it would sign the protocol but has deferred its signature.

Central Asian Nuclear Weapons Free Zone

Signed on September 8, 2006, this treaty creates a NWFZ in the five Central Asian states of Kazakhstan, Kyrgyzstan, Tajikistan, Turkmenistan, and Uzbekistan. With Kazakhstan's ratification in January 2009, all five countries have joined the treaty.

The treaty entered into force on March 21, 2009. This treaty is the first nuclear weapon-free zone located entirely in the northern hemisphere, and prohibits the development, manufacture, stockpiling, acquisition, or possession of any nuclear explosive device within the zone.

The treaty requires signatories to accept enhanced IAEA safeguards on nuclear material and activities, addresses the impact of production and testing of Soviet nuclear weapons on the environment, and implements measures to meet international standards for nuclear facility security.

Other Agreements

The United States has concluded arrangements with several states on a bilateral basis and on a multilateral basis in an effort to address specific proliferation challenges. In 1994, the United States signed the Agreed Framework with North Korea (which was terminated in 2003) and now addresses the North Korean nuclear program through the Six Party Talks. The United States addresses the Iranian nuclear program with the other permanent members of the U.N. Security Council plus Germany in the "P-5+1" Contact Group. The United States also provides bilateral assistance to countries to secure their WMD-relevant materials and technologies, or to detect their movement across borders.

In 2002, the United States initiated a "10 plus 10 over 10" effort within the G-8 to provide additional funding for nonproliferation assistance to Russia and the newly independent states of the former Soviet Union (NIS), called the G-8 Global Partnership Against the Spread of Weapons and Materials of Mass Destruction. The United States also created the Proliferation Security Initiative in 2003 to improve coordination on WMD interdiction efforts. The U.S.-Russian-led Global Initiative to Combat Nuclear Terrorism also aims to guide and coordinate international activities. The establishment of these joint activities reflected a trend away from internationally negotiated approaches to proliferation controls and towards ad hoc cooperation amongst "like-minded states," at least during the Bush administration's tenure, and due to heightened perception of WMD threats following the attacks of September 11, 2001.

G-8 Global Partnership

At a summit held in June 2002 in Kananaskis, Canada, G-8 members agreed to a Global Partnership to halt the spread of weapons of mass destruction and related materials and technology. The G-8 members agreed to raise $20 billion over 10 years in nonproliferation— related assistance beginning Russia, of which the United States committed to providing $10B. Projects relating to disarmament, nonproliferation, counterterrorism and nuclear safety initially were to focus on Russia. Russia and, since 2004, Ukraine are the official recipients of Global Partnership funds. Since 2002, 12 countries and the European Union have joined the G-8 as donors. The four priority areas of work as identified at the Kananaskis Summit are (1) destruction of chemical weapons, (2) dismantlement of decommissioned nuclear submarines, (3) disposition of fissile materials, and (4) employment of former weapons scientists. Some donor countries also emphasize the importance of biological weapons-related and nuclear material security assistance.

A G8 Global Partnership Working Group meets regularly to coordinate assistance efforts, and publishes a report and annex detailing projects at the summit each year.[17]

At the June 2004 Sea Island summit, the Global Partnership states agreed to consider expanding assistance to states outside the former Soviet Union. At their 2008 and 2009 summits, the G-8 countries agreed to extend the Global Partnership to recipients worldwide on a case-by-case basis. This would mirror U.S. efforts to expand its own cooperative threat reduction assistance to states outside of Russia and the former Soviet Union, for example, Albania. Outside observers assess that pledges are about $2 billion short of the $20 billion goal, and there remains a gap between pledges and actual funds spent. The Global Partnership is expected to be a main focus of the G8 Summit in 2010, as the initiative nears its 10-year anniversary and since Canada holds the G-8 presidency.

Global Partnership countries will be examining whether and how to extend the initiative beyond its first 10 years. The U.S. government supports the further expansion of Global Partnership recipients and an extension of the effort beyond 2012.

Global Initiative to Combat Nuclear Terrorism

At the July 2006 summit, the United States and Russia launched another initiative—the Global Initiative to Combat Nuclear Terrorism. As of July 2008, 76 states have agreed to the statement of principles and are Global Initiative partner nations. The International Atomic Energy Agency (IAEA), the European Union (EU) and International Criminal Police Organization (INTERPOL) have observer status.

Although it does not receive funding of its own, the initiative appears to exceed the G-8 Global Partnership in its scope. Participating states share a common goal to improve national capabilities to combat nuclear terrorism by sharing best practices through multinational exercises and expert level meetings.

Without dues or a secretariat, actions under the Initiative will take legal guidance from the International Convention on the Suppression of Acts of Nuclear Terrorism, the Convention on the Physical Protection of Nuclear Materials and its amendment, and U.N. Security Council Resolutions 1540 and 1373.[18] According to a White House fact sheet issued at the time of its announcement, the initiative has the following goals:[19]

- Improve security of nuclear material and radioactive substances and nuclear facilities;
- Detect and prevent illicit trafficking in such materials, especially by terrorists;
- Develop responses to nuclear terrorist attacks;
- Cooperate in developing technical means to combat nuclear terrorism;
- Take all possible measures to deny safe haven to terrorists seeking to acquire or use nuclear materials; and
- Strengthen national legal frameworks to ensure the effective prosecution of terrorists.

Global Initiative partner nations met in June 2009 in the Hague to discuss "enhancing international partnerships by sharing best practices." In past meetings the partner countries have focused on strengthening detection and forensics; denying safe haven and financing to terrorists; deterring terrorist intentions to acquire and use nuclear devices. Participants have developed "Model Nuclear Detection Guidelines." An International Nuclear Terrorism Law Enforcement Conference, organized by the FBI, was held in Miami in June 2007 for Global Initiative partners. Tabletop and field exercises are held to identify and address individual states' vulnerabilities. According to a State Department fact sheet, over 30 workshops and exercises have been held since the initiative began.[20] President Obama proposed in an April 2009 speech in Prague that the Global Initiative should become a "durable, international institution" but it is not yet clear how this will be carried out.

Proliferation Security Initiative[21]

President Bush announced the Proliferation Security Initiative (PSI) in May 2003 to improve multilateral cooperation in interdicting shipments of weapons of mass destruction-related materials and delivery systems at sea, on land, and in the air. U.S. officials stress that PSI is a voluntary effort consistent with national legal authorities and international law. The stated purpose is to strengthen the enforcement of already-existing export controls associated with nonproliferation treaties, and to better coordinate interdiction efforts through multilateral training exercises. States agreed to a set of interdiction principles in Paris in September 2003 and 90 nations now support PSI. PSI participants conduct joint interdiction training exercises and hold regular operational experts working group meetings. The United States is pursuing the conclusion of ship-boarding agreements with key states that have high volumes of

Proliferation Control Regimes: Background and Status   23

international shipping. The United States has signed such agreements with the Bahamas, Belize, Croatia, Cyprus, Liberia, Malta, the Marshall Islands, Mongolia, and Panama. The Obama administration has given full support to PSI and has said it wants to strengthen and "institutionalize" the effort.[22]

U.N. Security Council Resolution 1540

In April 2004, the U.N. Security Council adopted Resolution 1540, which requires all states to "criminalize proliferation, enact strict export controls and secure all sensitive materials within their borders." UNSCR 1540 called on states to enforce effective domestic controls over WMD and WMD-related materials in production, use, storage, and transport; to maintain effective border controls; and to develop national export and trans-shipment controls over such items, all of which should help interdiction efforts. The resolution did not, however, provide any enforcement authority, nor did it specifically mention interdiction. About two-thirds of all states have reported to the U.N. on their efforts to strengthen defenses against WMD trafficking. U.N. Security Council Resolutions 1673 (2006) and 1810 (2008) extended the duration of the 1540 Committee.

The committee is currently focused on identifying assistance projects for states in need and matching donors to improve these WMD controls.

Implementing the Regime

Although the Nuclear Nonproliferation Treaty (NPT) is perhaps the most visible aspect of the nuclear nonproliferation regime, the success of nonproliferation efforts relies on the sturdy functioning of national export control laws and their implementation, the Zangger Committee and Nuclear Suppliers Group multilateral coordination of export controls, and effective inspections conducted by the International Atomic Energy Agency (IAEA). Equally important is the *quid pro quo* of technical assistance in the peaceful uses of nuclear energy that the IAEA provides.

The International Atomic Energy Agency (IAEA)

The IAEA, a U.N.-affiliated international organization, was established in 1957 to "accelerate and enlarge the contribution of atomic energy to peace, health and prosperity," and to ensure "that assistance provided by it ... is not used in such a way as to further any military purpose."[23] With the entry into force of the NPT in 1970, it performs the dual missions of verifying NPT obligations and providing assistance in peaceful nuclear technology to developing nations. By December 2009, the agency had 151 member states and an annual budget of about $400 million.[24] The IAEA safeguards system monitors nuclear materials and technology to deter and detect diversions from peaceful to military uses.

The administrative structure of the agency resembles that of the United Nations. The General Conference includes all members and meets annually. The Board of Governors has 35 members, nine of which are permanent advanced nuclear nations, with the remaining board members serving one-year terms as representatives of regional nuclear interests. The Secretariat is the administrative arm of the agency. It is headed by the director general, who is the chief policy-making official. The current director general, Yukiya Amano, is a Japanese diplomat. The IAEA won the Nobel Peace Prize in 2005 under its previous director general, Mohamed El Baradei.

In over 25 years of inspections, five states have been declared in violation of their safeguards agreements: Iraq, North Korea, Romania, Libya, and Iran. Following revelations in 1991 of Iraq's clandestine activities, the IAEA developed a strengthened safeguards program (formerly called "93+2") to improve its ability to detect unreported nuclear activities in non-weapons states. The program includes

- provision of intelligence information to the IAEA by member states about suspect nuclear activities;
- access for inspectors to any location on a timely basis;
- new safeguards technology;
- measures to promote complete transparency and reporting of all nuclear commerce;
- sufficient financial resources to carry out the IAEA's expanded responsibilities.

State parties to the NPT have been required to ratify new "model protocol" agreements to their existing nuclear safeguards agreements with the IAEA (INFCIRC/540). President Bush submitted the U.S. model protocol agreement to the Senate for its consent to ratification in 2002. The Senate gave its advice and consent to the protocol on March 31, 2004 (Treaty Doc. 107-7, Senate Executive Report 108-12). On December 18, 2006, implementing legislation was passed in P.L. 109-401, as part of the Hyde Act. On December 30, 2008, the president signed the instrument of ratification for the Additional Protocol. It was deposited with the IAEA and entered into force on January 6,

Proliferation Control Regimes: Background and Status 25

2009. A continuing issue will be adequate funding for the IAEA safeguards. The annual safeguards budget is insufficient to carry out the IAEA's new responsibilities; the agency relies on extrabudgetary (voluntary) contributions to fully fund its work. Thus, the IAEA's ability to carry out its growing responsibilities and efforts to upgrade its safeguards system continue to be limited by members' reluctance to increase the IAEA regular budget. The United States had advocated for increasing the budget of the IAEA.

Since September 11, 2001, the IAEA has been promoting efforts to help prevent terrorists from acquiring or using weapons of mass destruction, including nuclear or radiological devices. These have focused primarily on upgrading its assistance in physical security, in locating orphaned radioactive sources, and in promoting enhancement of the Convention on the Protection of Physical Security. The IAEA established a Code of Conduct on the Safety and Security of Radioactive Sources in 2001 and an Action Plan on Combating Nuclear Terrorism in 2002. In 2005, the IAEA Board of Governors adopted a four-year Nuclear Security Plan 2006-2009.[25] In 2009, a Nuclear Security Action Plan for 2010-2013 was outlined. The Nuclear Security Fund (NSF) is a voluntary funding mechanism to support activities to prevent, detect, and respond to nuclear terrorism. Implementation of the Nuclear Security Plan is dependent on contributions to the NSF.[26] As of September 2009, 107 states participate in the IAEA's Illicit Trafficking Database, which facilitates the exchange of information related to the illicit trafficking of nuclear or radiological material.

In response to revelations in 2004 about Pakistani scientist A.Q. Khan's clandestine nuclear sales to Libya, Iran, and North Korea, the IAEA's director general proposed seven steps to enhance the nuclear nonproliferation regime. These include a five-year moratorium on construction of uranium enrichment and plutonium reprocessing facilities; conversion of nuclear reactors using highly enriched uranium (HEU) to low-enriched uranium; making the Additional Protocol the verification norm of the NPT; revisiting U.N. Security Council actions in response to a state's withdrawal from the NPT; universal implementation of U.N. Security Council Resolution 1540; acceleration of Article VI actions by nuclear weapons states (toward nuclear disarmament); and resolution of regional security tensions that give rise to proliferation, including a Middle East nuclear-weapon-free zone.[27] Measures to further strengthen the non-proliferation aspects of the IAEA's work meet resistant by member states who are more concerned about access to peaceful use of nuclear technology. In particular, the case of Iran's noncompliance with its safeguards obligations continues to present challenges for the IAEA and the nonproliferation regime.

The Nuclear Suppliers Group (NSG)

In 1971, a group of seven NPT nuclear supplier nations formed the Nuclear Exporters Committee, known as the Zangger Committee, to assist in restricting nuclear trade as called for in Article III of the NPT.[28] In 1974, the Zangger Committee compiled a list of nuclear export items that could be potentially useful for military applications of nuclear technology. The nuclear suppliers agreed that the transfer of items on the list would "trigger" a requirement for IAEA safeguards to ensure that the items were not used to make nuclear explosives. The Zangger list included reactors, reactor components, and certain nuclear materials such as heavy water. In recent years, the list of controlled items has been expanded and updated. Membership is voluntary and implies no formal commitments for enforcement of the guidelines. As of January 2010, the Zangger Committee had 37 members,[29] including all five NPT-recognized nuclear weapon states. The committee meets twice each year to exchange information and upgrade its list of controlled commodities.

Shaken by the 1974 test of a nuclear explosive device by India, the major nuclear suppliers in 1975 established a set of unpublished nuclear export guidelines.[30] In 1978, the group, known as the London Club, added new members and announced a common policy regarding nuclear exports. While the NPT's Zangger list initially included only nuclear materials and components used directly in weapons development, the London Club adopted more restrictive export control guidelines that included some dual-use items, with civil and military applications. The NSG guidelines called for suppliers to exercise restraint regarding transfers of enrichment and reprocessing technology, and required the provision of physical security for transferred nuclear facilities and materials, acceptance of safeguards on replicated facilities (based on a design transferred from a London Club member-state), and prohibitions against retransfer of nuclear exports to third parties.

Although NSG guidelines were in place, members took no further actions until 1991. Concerned about Iraq's successful procurement of dual-use items and apparently inconsistent enforcement of nuclear export controls in several supplier countries, the NSG convened in March 1991 for the first time since 1978 to update its list of controlled commodities. The expanded group agreed on new guidelines in January 1992 for transfers of a wider range of nuclear-related, dual-use equipment, material and technology and jointly adopted the long-standing U.S. policy of requiring full-scope safeguards for all nuclear exports. (Nations purchasing nuclear technology must open *all* nuclear facilities to inspection, not just the facility in which an imported item is used.)[31] The NSG has expanded to 45 members.[32]

Some developing nations have objected to the NSG because it further divides the technologically advanced nuclear "haves" from the "have nots" and creates additional obstacles to their access to nuclear technology. A few countries have turned to suppliers outside of the NSG to avoid the requirement for full-scope safeguards on nuclear exports. The emergence of new nuclear suppliers that do not subscribe to NSG guidelines undermines the efforts of NSG members to control the spread of nuclear weapons.

The strengthening of NSG export policy after the Gulf War responded to numerous examples of illegal, covert, and suspicious nuclear trade involving Western firms and countries such as India, Iraq, Iran, Israel, Pakistan, Brazil, Argentina, South Africa, and others. These transfers underscored the limitations of voluntary export controls, but they also motivated U.S. officials to push for further tightening of NSG restrictions on world nuclear exports. However, as a voluntary association, the NSG has no formal administrative structure, no legal authority to influence the nuclear trade policies of its members, and no formal enforcement mechanism.

In 2005, the United States approached the NSG to create an exception for India to the NSG's requirement for full-scope safeguards as a condition of nuclear supply. Such an exception was necessary for the United States to implement its proposed civil nuclear cooperation initiative with India.[33] Key NSG members, such as the United States, Russia, and France, supported a country-specific exception, while other members questioned whether such an approach might be damaging to the nonproliferation regime. India and the IAEA formulated an India-specific safeguards agreement, as required by the Henry J. Hyde United States-India Peaceful Atomic Energy Cooperation Act of 2006 (P.L. 109-401) in 2008. In September 2008, the NSG agreed to exempt India from the full-scope safeguards requirement, although retained a policy of restraint on the transfer enrichment and reprocessing equipment. NSG members are discussing whether or not to adopt additional guidelines that would define eligibility criteria for the transfer of enrichment and reprocessing technologies to new states.

U.S. Government Organization

The Departments of State, Energy, Defense, Treasury, and Commerce, and the intelligence community are all involved in the formulation and implementation of nonproliferation policy.[34] Congress mandated the creation of a White House Coordinator for the Prevention of Weapons of Mass Destruction Proliferation and Terrorism (P.L. 110-53). The administration pledged to appoint "a deputy national security advisor to be in charge of coordinating all U.S. programs aimed at reducing the risk of nuclear terrorism and weapons proliferation."[35] Gary Samore was assigned this post, as National Security Council Coordinator for Arms Control and Nonproliferation. Primary functions of the various federal agencies are outlined below.

- The National Security Council coordinates nonproliferation, counterproliferation, threat reduction, and WMD terrorism prevention policy.
- The State Department, in consultation with the Energy Department, negotiates U.S. agreements for nuclear cooperation and arms control measures, represents U.S. nonproliferation interests with other states and international organizations such as the IAEA, and administers some nonproliferation assistance programs. The State Department also represents the United States and plans international coordination meetings for the G8 Global Partnership, Global Initiative to Combat Nuclear Terrorism, and Proliferation Security Initiative.
- The Department of Defense is responsible for counterproliferation strategy and policy, administers the Cooperative Threat Reduction (CTR) programs, and is involved in operational aspects of the Proliferation Security Initiative.
- The Department of Energy's National Nuclear Security administration provides technical expertise in nuclear weapons to support nonproliferation policy and diplomacy, largely through its national laboratories. DOE also administers nonproliferation programs to control fissile material in the former Soviet Union and elsewhere, the Global Threat Reduction Initiative and export control and border security programs.
- The Nuclear Regulatory Commission licenses nuclear exports subject to concurrence by the Department of State.
- The Department of Commerce oversees licensing of dual-use exports as mandated by Section 309(c) of the Nuclear Non-proliferation Act, which requires controls on "all export items, other than those licensed by the NRC, which could be, if used for purposes other than those for which the export is intended, of significance for nuclear explosive purposes."

Proliferation Control Regimes: Background and Status

- The Department of the Treasury oversees U.S. embargoes through its Office of Foreign Assets Control, and enforces export control through the U.S. Customs Service. It also represents the United States in the inter-governmental Financial Action Task Force (FATF).
- The Director of National Intelligence has a National Counterproliferation Center (NCPC) that coordinates intelligence on proliferation issues within the intelligence community.
- The Federal Bureau of Investigation (FBI) has a WMD Directorate.
- Several interagency working groups coordinate the various responsibilities for nonproliferation policy.

Since September 11, 2001, significant U.S. government interest has focused on counterproliferation programs—that is, military measures against weapons of mass destruction. Although the Department of Defense has had programs in place for several years, efforts in this area have been renewed. Counterproliferation includes active and passive defenses to protect U.S. and allied troops. The December 2002 National Strategy to Combat Weapons of Mass Destruction described counterproliferation as including interdiction, deterrence, defense, and mitigation.[36] Preemption is explicitly described as an option under defense and mitigation policies. Increased attention has also been given to breaking down proliferation finance networks. U.S. government agencies have also stepped up efforts to secure or remove nuclear and radiological materials worldwide and to improve detection of WMD-related trafficking at borders. President Obama has pledged to secure all vulnerable nuclear materials around the world in four years. A Global Nuclear Security Summit will be held in April 2010 to further this goal.

U.S. Laws[37]

The main legislative pillars of U.S. nuclear nonproliferation policy are the Atomic Energy Act of 1954, as amended by the Nuclear Nonproliferation Act of 1978, and the Arms Export Control Act of 1968.

The Atomic Energy Act of 1954 (AEA)[38]

The Atomic Energy Act of 1954 established legal authority for the commercial and military development of nuclear energy. It gave primary authority for the development and oversight of the U.S. government's nuclear programs to a civilian agency: the Atomic Energy Commission (now the

Nuclear Regulatory Commission). In 1974, these duties were divided between the NRC and the Department of Energy. A major purpose of the act was to establish controls on the export of nuclear materials, goods, information, and technology. Under the AEA, the State Department must negotiate an agreement for nuclear cooperation as a precondition for exports of sensitive U.S. nuclear technology to any foreign country. Each agreement must meet several standards outlined in the AEA. Moreover, the act contains penalties and restrictions for countries that do not uphold the terms of nuclear agreements with the United States. Congress reviews all such agreements before they can enter into force.

The Nuclear Non-Proliferation Act of 1978 (NNPA)[39]

Congress and the Carter administration viewed U.S. leadership and control over the international nuclear fuel cycle as an effective means of restraining the spread of uranium enrichment and plutonium reprocessing facilities throughout the world. Enrichment and reprocessing technologies are key technologies for states aspiring to develop nuclear weapons. While reaffirming the U.S. commitment to be a reliable supplier of nuclear technology and fuels, the act established an important new requirement for nations importing U.S. nuclear technology and materials: they must accept full-scope safeguards on their entire nuclear program. This standard was adopted by NSG members in 1992. The act also established a requirement of prior U.S. approval for retransfers or reprocessing of material or equipment as well as to material produced using U.S.- exported technology. These measures gave the United States much more control over the foreign uses of U.S.-origin nuclear material.

Title III of the NNPA includes such varied measures as requiring the Department of Energy to obtain NRC licenses to distribute source and special material and establishment of criteria for terminating nuclear exports from the United States (which affects bilateral nuclear cooperation agreements) to include detonation of a nuclear device, termination/abrogation or violation of IAEA safeguards, or engaging in activities involving nuclear material which have significance in the manufacture of nuclear explosive devices (covering a wide array of activities). Additional prohibited acts included violating a nuclear cooperation agreement with the United States; assisting a non-nuclear-weapon state in activities involving nuclear material that could potentially help in the manufacture or acquisition of a nuclear explosive device; or enriching any U.S. source or special material without the permission of the United

States. The NNPA requires (in Section 601) the president to report annually to Congress on the government's efforts to prevent nuclear proliferation.

The Arms Export Control Act (AECA)[40]

The Arms Export Control Act (AECA), as amended, authorizes U.S. government military sales, loans, leases, financing, and licensing of commercial arms sales to other countries. The AECA coordinates such actions with other foreign policy considerations, including nonproliferation, and determines eligibility of recipients for military exports, sales, leases, loans, and financing.

- *Section 3(f) (22 USC. 2753(f))* prohibits U.S. military sales or leases to any country that the president determines is in material breach of binding commitments to the United States under international treaties or agreements regarding nonproliferation of nuclear explosive devices and unsafeguarded special nuclear material.
- *Section 40 (22 USC. 2780)* prohibits exports or assistance in exporting (financial or otherwise) munitions to countries that provide support for terrorism. Included in the definition of acts of international terrorism are: "all activities that the Secretary [of State] determines willfully aid or abet the international proliferation of nuclear explosive devices to individuals or groups or willfully aid or abet an individual or groups in acquiring unsafeguarded special nuclear material." The president can rescind a determination or waive sanctions if essential to the national security interests of the United States.
- *Section 101 (22 USC. 2799aa)* (formerly section 669 of the Foreign Assistance Act) prohibits foreign economic or military assistance to countries that deliver or receive nuclear enrichment equipment, materials, or technology unless the supplier agrees to place such under safeguards and the recipient has full-scope safeguards. The president, who makes the determination, can waive sanctions if they will have a serious adverse effect on vital U.S. interests, given assurances that the recipient will not acquire, develop, or assist others in acquiring or developing nuclear weapons.
- *Section 102 (22 USC. 2799aa-1)* (formerly section 670 of the Foreign Assistance Act) prohibits foreign economic or military assistance to countries that deliver or receive nuclear reprocessing equipment,

material, or technology to or from another country; or any non-nuclear-weapon state which illegally exports from the United States items that would contribute to nuclear proliferation. The president, who makes the determination, can waive the sanction if he finds that ending assistance would adversely affect U.S. nonproliferation objectives or jeopardize the common defense and security. The section further prohibits assistance (except humanitarian or food assistance), defense sales, export licenses for U.S. Munitions List items, other export licenses subject to foreign policy controls, and various credits and loans to any country that the president has determined transfers a nuclear explosive device, design information, or component to a non-nuclear-weapons state, or is a non-nuclear-weapons state and receives a nuclear device, design information, or component, or detonates a nuclear explosive device.

Much of the language on nuclear nonproliferation controls that had been incorporated into the Foreign Assistance Act earlier (including the 1977 Glenn-Symington amendments on enrichment and reprocessing and the 1985 Pressler amendment related to Pakistan) were incorporated into the AECA in 1994 by the Nuclear Proliferation Prevention Act (see discussion below).

Export Administration Act of 1979 (EAA)

The Export Administration Act of 1979 (P.L. 96-72) authorizes the executive branch to regulate private sector exports of particular goods and technology to other countries. Although the act expired in 1989, export controls have been implemented under executive orders and the International Emergency Economic Powers Act (IEEPA).[41] The EAA coordinates such actions with other foreign policy considerations, including nonproliferation, and determines eligibility of recipients for exports. *Section 5 (50 USC. app. 2404)* authorizes the president to curtail or prohibit the export of any goods or services for national security reasons: to comply with other laws regarding a potential recipient country's political status or political stability, to cooperate with international agreements or understandings, or to protect militarily critical technologies. *Section 6 (50 USC. app. 2405)* authorizes the president to curtail or prohibit the export of goods or services for foreign policy reasons. Within Section 6, for example, *Section 6(j)* establishes the State Department's list of countries found to be supporting acts of international terrorism, a list on which many other restrictions and prohibitions in law are based.

Export-Import Bank Act of 1945

The Export-Import Bank Act of 1945 (P.L. 79-173) establishes the Export-Import Bank of the United States and authorizes the Bank to finance and facilitate exports and imports and the exchange of commodities and services between the United States and foreign countries. Key nuclear-nonproliferation-related provisions were added in 1978. These include *Section 2(b)(1)(B) (12 USC. 635(b)(1)(B))* and *Section 2(b)(4) (12 USC. 635(b)(4))*, which together allow the Bank to deny credit generally if that credit does not help advance U.S. nuclear proliferation policy, and specifically, if a person or country has (1) violated, abrogated or terminated a nuclear safeguards agreements; (2) violated a nuclear cooperation agreement with the United States; or (3) aided or abetted a non-nuclear-weapon state to acquire a nuclear explosive device or to acquire unsafeguarded special nuclear material. There is a provision for presidential waiver. (See *Appendix B* for details.)

The Export-Import Bank Act of 1945 was amended in 2002[42] to allow denial of Ex-Im Bank financing for violations of the Foreign Corrupt Practices Act, the Arms Export Control Act, the International Emergency Economic Powers Act, or the Export Administration Act of 1979, extending its purview from strictly nuclear to CW, BW, and missile-related concerns.

Nuclear Proliferation Prevention Act of 1994

In 1994 Congress approved the Nuclear Proliferation Prevention Act (NPPA, Title VIII, of the Foreign Relations Authorization Act, Fiscal Years 1994 and 1995, P.L. 103-236), which primarily strengthened penalties against persons who aid or abet the acquisition of nuclear weapons or unsafeguarded nuclear weapons materials, or countries (non-nuclear-weapon states) that obtain or explode nuclear devices. Sanctions include cutoff of U.S. assistance, prohibition on involvement with U.S. government procurement, stringent licensing requirements for technology exports, and opposition to loans or credits from international financial institutions. These sanctions were imposed on India and Pakistan following their nuclear tests in May 1998, but were gradually relaxed. Legislation passed in the 106th Congress extended the president's authority to relax sanctions on India and Pakistan for a year, and the Senate passed a bill suspending sanctions on the two countries for five years.

The FY2000 Department of Defense Appropriations bill (P.L. 106-79) extended the authority to suspend sanctions. Following the September 11 terrorist attacks, President Bush lifted all remaining sanctions on India and Pakistan in response to support of U.S. operations in Afghanistan.

The NPPA defined for the first time in U.S. law the term "nuclear explosive device." It defined "terrorism" as used in the AECA, to include activities that assist groups or individuals to acquire any nuclear explosive device. It included a sense of Congress that identified 24 measures to strengthen IAEA safeguards, some of which have been implemented. Relevant sections include *Section 821 (22 USC. 3201 note)*, which requires U.S. government procurement sanctions; *Section 823 (22 USC. 3201 note)*, which requires U.S. executive directors of international financial institutions to vote against finance that might promote nuclear proliferation; and *Section 824 (22 USC. 3201 note)*, which takes aim at financial institutions and persons involved with financial institutions from assisting nuclear proliferation through the provision of financing. (See *Appendix B* for specific details.)

Nunn-Lugar/Cooperative Threat Reduction Program Legislation

In late 1991, Congress passed the Soviet Nuclear Threat Reduction Act (which became known as the Nunn-Lugar Amendment), establishing programs to assist with the safe and secure storage and dismantlement of nuclear weapons in Russia and the Newly Independent States (NIS). These programs initially focused on the "loose nukes" problem, but have broadened their focus to address a variety of proliferation risks associated with weak political control over nuclear materials, equipment, and expertise, as well as CW, BW, and missiles. This effort has expanded to include the CTR program in DOD and nonproliferation programs in DOE and the State Department.[43] The FY2008 defense authorization bill expanded the program to countries outside the former Soviet Union, and eliminated the annual certification requirements for the CTR program.[44]

Iran-Iraq Arms Nonproliferation Act of 1992

Section 1602 of the Defense Authorization for FY1993 (Title XVI, P.L. 102-484, as amended) extended existing sanctions on Iraq to Iran. The law states that it is the policy of the United States to oppose any transfer to Iran or Iraq that could contribute to either country's ability to acquire nuclear, chemical, biological, or advanced conventional weapons. *Section 1604* requires the president to impose sanctions against any person whom he has determined to be engaged in such transfers. *Section 1605* similarly addresses activities of foreign governments. The 104th Congress amended the law (by passage of section 1408(a), P.L. 104-106, National Defense Authorization Act for Fiscal Year 1996) to make it apply to transfers contributing to the development of weapons of mass destruction as well as advanced conventional weapons.

Iran, North Korea and Syria Nonproliferation Act

The law (P.L. 106-178) imposes penalties on countries whose companies help Iran's efforts to acquire weapons of mass destruction and missile delivery systems. In 2005, P.L. 109-112, Iran Nonproliferation Amendments Act, added Syria to the law and added sanctions for transfers to and from those countries. In 2006, Congress also added North Korea to the Act (P.L. 109-353).

Foreign Operations, Export Financing, and Related Programs Appropriations Act of 2006

This law (P.L. 109-102) withheld 60% of funds set aside for assistance to the Russian government until the president certifies that assistance to Iran has ceased. Assistance constitutes technical training, expertise, technology, or equipment needed to build a nuclear reactor, develop research facilities or programs, or ballistic missile technologies.

Issues for the 111th Congress

Since September 11, 2001, much of Congress's attention in the area of the nonproliferation of weapons of mass destruction has focused on how to mitigate the threat U.S. citizens face right now—improving domestic preparedness against WMD terrorism and improving intelligence capabilities to detect evidence of proliferation-related activities. Above all, however, most experts agree that the U.S. government should continue to address nuclear proliferation at the source— that is, securing nuclear materials and halting information flows from WMD-knowledgeable scientists to countries of proliferation concern.

Other key nuclear nonproliferation issues for Congress include:

- facilitating implementation of DOD's Cooperative Threat Reduction and relevant DOE programs that improve controls on nuclear materials, equipment, and expertise in Russia and the NIS and expanding these efforts to countries outside the NIS;

- monitoring efforts to end Pyongyang's nuclear weapons program;
- monitoring Iran's nuclear program, including Russian and Chinese nuclear exports and assistance;
- opposing the nuclear arms race between India and Pakistan, preventing those countries from exporting WMD technology and cooperating to prevent terrorist access to their facilities;
- strengthening the IAEA safeguards system to enforce the NPT and prevent further proliferation;
- maintaining and expanding adherence to NSG nuclear export control standards;
- curbing dangerous Chinese and Russian nuclear exports;
- banning the production of fissile material for nuclear weapons;
- consideration of the future of the U.S. nuclear arsenal and impact of these policies on nonproliferation.

Closer to home, Congress will be asked to consider how to dispose of tons of excess plutonium from dismantled Russian and U.S. warheads without increasing proliferation risks; and how U.S. arms control and defense cooperation (particularly missile defense cooperation) might affect proliferation risks.

Congress will also be asked to assess U.S. and multilateral programs to lessen the proliferation risks of an expansion of nuclear energy. Congress may also exert oversight over key nonproliferation programs, such as Proliferation Security Initiative and the Global Threat Reduction Initiative.

CHEMICAL AND BIOLOGICAL WEAPONS PROLIFERATION REGIME[45]

Prohibitions against the use of chemical weapons date back to the International Peace Conferences that met at the Hague in 1899 and 1907; these pre-World War I prohibitions were reaffirmed in the 1919 Versailles Treaty and further expanded in the 1925 Geneva Protocol.

In some ways, it is more difficult to prevent the proliferation of these weapons than nuclear weapons because they require a smaller infrastructure and the production technologies are much more widely disseminated.

Furthermore, it is more difficult to distinguish between legitimate and illegitimate chemical and biological activities.[46] The regimes that have grown

Proliferation Control Regimes: Background and Status   37

up around these weapons include treaties, supplier agreements, and domestic laws.

Treaties and Agreements

The Chemical Weapons Convention (CWC) and the Biological and Toxin Weapons Convention (BWC) are the two primary treaties related to CBW proliferation. The United States is a state party to both the BWC and the CWC.

Chemical Weapons Convention (CWC)

Culminating 25 years of negotiations, the Chemical Weapons Convention opened for signature in January 1993.[47] The CWC entered into force on April 29, 1997. As of January 27, 2010, the treaty had 188 states-parties.[48]

The CWC prohibits the development, production, stockpiling, transfer, and use of chemical weapons. The convention mandates the destruction of chemical weapon arsenals within 10 years of its coming into force. The CWC also restricts the international transfer of chemicals deemed useful in the production of chemical weapons, so-called "precursors." Most precursor chemicals are dual-use, with legitimate peaceful applications. The CWC establishes extensive lists or "schedules" of precursors whose production, use, and transfer must be reported to the CWC's Organization for the Prohibition of Chemical Weapons (OPCW). The schedules are designated I-III, in order of their potential usefulness in chemical warfare. Schedule I chemicals may be exported only to states parties (i.e., nations that have ratified the CWC). In accordance with treaty provisions, as of April 2000, the export of Schedule II chemicals to non-states parties became prohibited.

Biological and Toxin Weapons Convention

The Biological Weapons Convention was concluded in 1972, with U.S. ratification and entry in force in 1975.[49] As of January 27, 2010, the convention had 163 states parties. The convention bans the development, production, and stockpiling of biological agents or toxins "of types and in quantities that have no justification for peaceful purposes." The development, manufacture, and possession of BW weapons or delivery systems is also prohibited. States parties also agree not to transfer biological agents or toxins for any but peaceful purposes.[50]

The United Kingdom first tabled a draft treaty in 1968 that contained verification provisions. Assuming the Soviet Union would reject such a proposal, the United States, with UK agreement, privately negotiated a treaty text with the Soviets that did not include a verification mechanism. On the same day in 1969, both the United States and the Soviet Union tabled identical draft treaties. In 1969, the United States declared a unilateral end to its offensive BW program and suggested separating the BW issue from the chemical-biological arms control negotiations in Geneva. Negotiations on this proposal took three years to conclude.

Implementing the Regime

International Organizations

The CBW nonproliferation regime relies on the Australia Group and the Organization for the Prohibition of Chemical Weapons (OPCW), which was created by the CWC. There is no independent international organization to administer the Biological Weapons Convention. Currently, BWC member states report all defensive biological activities to the United Nations Department of Disarmament Affairs. This information is reported to all BWC member states, with the State Department as the international point of contact within the U.S. government. The states-parties decided in December 2006 to establish an Implementation Support Unit for the BWC. According to its website, the three-person unit provides "administrative support and assistance; National Implementation support and assistance; Support and assistance for Confidence-Building Measures; and Support and assistance for obtaining universality."[51]

Australia Group (AG)

In 1984, United Nations investigators officially confirmed that chemical weapons had been used in the Iran-Iraq War. In response, the United States and several other countries began to implement export controls on chemicals that could be used to manufacture chemical weapons. In 1985, Australia proposed that concerned countries meet in order to coordinate their export controls and share information to enhance their effectiveness. The first meeting took place in June 1985, and biennial meetings continue at the Australian embassy in Paris.

The Australia Group has established a list of chemicals and equipment that are subject to control. In 1990, in response to growing concerns over the proliferation of covert biological weapons programs, certain biological agents and research/production equipment were added to the control list. Australia Group guidelines do not call for prohibiting the export of control list items, but rather establishing monitoring and licensing procedures, with export denial only if there is reason to suspect potential contribution to a CBW program. The group's list does not curtail legitimate trade. Since its inception, the Australia Group has added controls on the transfer of information and knowledge that could aid BW proliferation. These included "catch-all" constraints covering items that are not on control lists, adding eight toxins to the control list, adopting controls on technology associated with dual-use biological equipment, and agreeing to control intangible technology transfer (i.e., by phone, fax, or internet) that could be used to advance CBW programs.

As noted, the Australia Group does not have an independent administrative organization. National governments administer their own export control programs. As an informal effort, it is not based on international treaty, is not affiliated with any international organization, and has no independent administrative structure. It operates entirely upon consensus of its 41 members and its decisions are not binding. Countries are admitted to membership only upon the full consensus of current members, and must have demonstrated compliance with the CWC and BWC, and have an effective export control regime.

The question of the Australia Group's relationship to the Chemical Weapons Convention revolves around the convention's Article XI which declares that states parties will not

> maintain among themselves any restrictions, including those in any international agreements, incompatible with the obligations undertaken under this Convention, which would restrict or impede trade and the development and promotion of scientific and technological knowledge.

The Australia Group maintains that its export control regime is compatible with the objectives of the convention, and therefore not prohibited. A number of developing countries, led by Iran (a CWC state party), maintain that the AG controls should be dropped—particularly for CWC states parties. They view the controls as a tool of economic oppression on the part of developed countries, even though no country has been able to provide an example where AG controls have resulted in a denial of exports for legitimate purposes.

Organization for the Prohibition of Chemical Weapons (OPCW)

The OPCW is headquartered in The Hague. It has four components:

- Conference of States Parties—Comprises all nations who have ratified the convention; meets annually; has the responsibility to ensure compliance and levy sanctions; selects the Executive Council;
- Executive Council—Comprises 41 states parties on a two-year rotation[52]; directs the routine administration of the OPCW;
- Technical Secretariat—Comprises a permanent international work force; administers and monitors treaty compliance (inspections, data collection and assessment);
- Scientific Advisory Board—Comprised of independent experts to advise the OPCW on relevant scientific and technical issues.

U.S. Government Organizations

In the United States, the following offices, among others, participate in administering the CBW export control program, with State serving as the international point of contact:

- Department of Commerce—Under Secretary of Commerce, Bureau of Industry and Security;
- Department of State—Under Secretary for Arms Control and International Security—Bureau of International Security and Nonproliferation administers the CWC and export controls;
- Department of Defense—Deputy Under Secretary for Technology Security Policy and Counterproliferation;
- The Department of the Treasury oversees U.S. embargoes through its Office of Foreign Assets Control;
- The Department of Homeland Security enforces export control through the U.S. Customs Service.

U.S. Laws[53]

U.S. laws pertaining to chemical and biological weapons proliferation include statutes and executive orders, the most important of which are the Export Administration Act and the Arms Export Control Act. These statutes operate on the principle that licenses are required for the export of certain goods, and that it is government policy to deny such licenses if there is a danger that the items will contribute to CBW proliferation.

Export Administration Act of 1979

(P.L. 96-72, Section 6(m) and 11C, 50 USC. App. 2405m and 2410c). This act requires a license for the export of dual-use goods or technology that "would directly and substantially" assist CBW proliferation. Under the act, the Secretary of Commerce maintains a list of such goods. Exports to countries which have entered into an agreement for the control of restricted goods (i.e., Australia Group members) are exempted from licensing requirements. The EAA requires the president to impose procurement and import sanctions on foreign persons who contribute to CBW proliferation through exports.

Arms Export Control Act

Section 81 of the AECA (22 USC. 2798) provides the State Department the authority to maintain licensing of the export of chemical and biological agents and munitions. It also provides criminal penalties for violation and specifies sanctions against foreign persons who contribute to CW or BW proliferation through exports, and against countries which use chemical or biological weapons or make substantial preparations to do so.

Chemical and Biological Weapons Control and Warfare Elimination Act of 1991[54]

This act mandates U.S. sanctions, and encourages international sanctions, against countries that use chemical or biological weapons in violation of international law. *Section 307 (22 USC. 5605)* requires the president to terminate foreign assistance (except humanitarian, food, and agricultural assistance) arms sales and licenses, credits, guarantees, and certain exports to a government of a foreign country that he has determined has used or made substantial preparation to use chemical or biological weapons. Within three months, the president must determine and certify to Congress that the government: is no longer using chemical or biological weapons in violation of international law, is no longer using such weapons against its own people, has provided credible assurances that such behavior will not resume, and is willing to cooperate with U.N. or other international observers to verify that biological and chemical weapons are not still in use. Without this three-month determination, sanctions are required affecting multilateral development bank loans, U.S. bank loans or credits, exports, imports, diplomatic relations, and aviation access to and from the United States. The president may lift the sanctions after a year, and may waive the imposition of these sanctions.

Biological Anti-Terrorism Act of 1989

This act (P.L. 101-298) implements the Biological Weapons Convention, providing criminal penalties for its violation. It does not amend either the Export Administration Act or the Arms Export Control Act.

Additional CW/BW Nonproliferation Policy Provisions in Legislation

Congress has expressed views on CW/BW nonproliferation policy and U.S. government organization to implement those policies in several other laws. CBW-related provisions have been included in the Iran-Iraq Arms Nonproliferation Act of 1992, the Freedom Support Act, and the Cooperative Threat Reduction Act. These and other provisions are listed in *Table 2.*

Issues for the 111th Congress

Export Controls

Effective export controls are generally viewed as critical tools to stem the proliferation of chemical and biological weapons. The 111th Congress may consider changes to the export control laws.

For example, on July 31, 2009, Representative Sherman introduced the Export Control Improvements Act (H.R. 3515), co-sponsored by Representative Manzullo and Representative A. Smith, which contains provisions on export controls enforcement, integration of export control data in the AES, and diversion control.[55]

In addition, the White House announced in August 2009 that it was beginning a "broad-based interagency process for reviewing the overall U.S. export control system." When evaluating proposals for changing export controls, Congress may consider potential implications for the multilateral proliferation control regimes.

U.S. Compliance with CWC

None of the six CWC states-parties that declared possession of chemical weapons destroyed their stocks by the original April 29, 2007, deadline. In July 2007, Albania became the first country to have destroyed its declared chemical weapons. South Korea became the second on July 10, 2008. India became the third on March 16, 2009.

Three other states—Libya, Russia, and the United States—have declared possession of such weapons and all three have stated their intentions to destroy them.

The United States has already destroyed all of its Category Three stockpile and has declared no Category Two weapons. However, it has encountered difficulties in destroying its Category One chemical weapons stockpile. In April 2006, the United States submitted a formal request to the OPCW chairman and director-general to extend Washington's final chemical weapons destruction deadline from April 2007 to April 29, 2012, the latest possible date allowed under the CWC.[56]

However, Ambassador Eric Javits, U.S. Permanent Representative to the OPCW, added that "we do not expect to be able to meet that deadline" because Washington had encountered "delays and difficulties" in destroying its stockpile.[57]

These delays have generally resulted from the need to meet state and federal environmental requirements and from both local and congressional concerns over the means of destruction.

Reinforcing Javits' statement, former Secretary of Defense Donald Rumsfeld notified Congress in April 2006 that destruction of the U.S. stockpile by the April 2012 deadline "was in doubt based on the current schedules, but that the Department of Defense [DOD] would continue requesting resources needed to complete destruction as close to the 2012 deadline as practicable."

Andrew Weber, Assistant Secretary of Defense for Nuclear and Chemical and Biological Defense Programs, told the OPCW November 30, 2009, that the United States has destroyed over 67% of its Category One stockpile.[58] Washington projects that its four operating destruction facilities[59] will have destroyed 90% of the total U.S. stockpile by 2017.[60]

Two other facilities under construction will destroy the remaining chemical agents stockpiles located at Pueblo, CO, and Lexington, KY. A 2007 estimate from the DOD Assembled Chemical Weapons Alternatives (ACWA) program stated that these stockpiles would be destroyed by 2020 and 2023, respectively.[61]

However, the 2008 Defense Appropriations Act (P.L. 110-116) required the Defense Department to "complete work on the destruction" of the U.S. chemical weapons stockpile by the 2012 deadline "and in no circumstances later than December 31, 2017."

Additionally, the National Defense Authorization Act for Fiscal Year 2008 (P.L. 110-181) required that the Secretary of Defense submit a report to Congress that includes a

> description of the options and alternatives for accelerating the completion of chemical weapons destruction at each such facility, particularly in time to meet the [CWC] destruction deadline of April 29, 2012 ... and by December 31, 2017.

That report, submitted in June 2008, compared three options for accelerating stockpile destruction, noting that "[t]here are no options to achieve 100 percent destruction of the national stockpile by 2012."[62] The three options were as follows:

- Provide schedule incentives authorized by Congress[63] to ensure that the operating sites complete the destruction of their stockpiles by 2012.
- Transport portions of the remaining stockpile to destruction facilities that are already operating.
- Accelerate the destruction schedule for the Colorado and Kentucky sites.

A May 2009 DOD report to Congress proposes that the Department "seek additional resources" to complete destruction of the Colorado stockpile by 2017 and the Kentucky stockpile by 2021.[64] The 2010 Department of Defense Appropriations Act enables the Department to meet this timetable.[65]

U.S. Funding for OPCW

Ambassador Robert Mikulak stated April 20, 2010, that earlier that month Washington had "authorized full payment of the outstanding balance of our 2010 assessed contribution to the OPCW," explaining that the United States had previously "split our payment: 30% of our assessment in the first part of the year and the remaining 70% in the last three months. However, we have now been able to regularize our payment schedule so that our full assessment can be paid in the first part of the year."

Some observers had argued that, because the U.S. assessment comprises a large percentage of the OPCW's budget, these late payments negatively affected the organization's financial planning. Moreover, the Conference of States Parties Convention recognized the "negative consequences of the late payment of assessed contributions on the operational activities" of the OCPW in a December 2009 statement.[66]

Biological Weapons Convention— U.S. Biodefense Programs

In conducting oversight, the 111th Congress may consider the issue of transparency in U.S. biodefense programs. Some observers have argued that these programs could create suspicions that the United States is conducting research related to biological weapons that is prohibited by the BWC.[67]

MISSILE PROLIFERATION CONTROL REGIME[68]

In the early 1980s, the United States and its allies heightened their concern over the spread of missiles as the advanced industrial nations' monopoly on missile technology gave way to a diffusion of missiles and missile technology throughout much of the world. In April 1987, the United States, Canada, France, West Germany, Italy, Japan, and the United Kingdom created the Missile Technology Control Regime (MTCR) to prevent the proliferation of missiles and unmanned aerial vehicles capable of delivering nuclear weapons. Today, 34 countries are formal partners in the MTCR.[69] Although there is no permanent secretariat or headquarters, the French Foreign Ministry acts as a central point of contact.

In addition, China, Israel, Romania, and the Slovak Republic have agreed to observe MTCR guidelines as "unilateral adherents." China's application for MTCR membership, submitted in 2004, remains under review by the MTCR member states. China officially reiterated its commitment to MTCR goals in February 2008. Israel completed a memorandum of understanding with the United States affirming its commitment to abide by MTCR guidelines. Under the U.S.-India nuclear agreement (U.S.-India 123 Agreement of October 2008), India will be required to adhere to MTCR guidelines. And in April 2009, Kazakhstan said it would consider joining the MTCR a foreign policy priority.

The regime is based on the premise that foreign acquisition and development of missiles can be delayed, made more difficult and expensive, and even prevented if major producers agree to control exports of missiles and the equipment and technology used in missile production. The MTCR is similar in this regard to the Nuclear Suppliers Group, the Australia Group, and the Wassenaar Arrangement. It differs from the nuclear and chemical nonproliferation regimes in that the MTCR is not supported by a treaty and has no international organization to verify or enforce compliance. Rather, the MTCR is a set of common export control guidelines adopted and administered independently by each of the partner nations through consensus.

The specific missile equipment and technology subject to the guidelines is described in an annex to the MTCR Guidelines and divided into two categories. Each of the member countries is to exercise particular restraint in considering transfers of items in Category I, which include complete rocket systems and unmanned air vehicle (UAV) systems capable of delivering a 500- kilogram (1,100-pound) payload to a range of 300 kilometers (186 miles) or more, and complete subsystems of such missiles and vehicles. There is a strong presumption by the MTCR to deny transfers of these systems and components. The guidelines further state that the transfer of Category I production facilities will not be authorized.

In addition, export restraints are to be applied to Category II items, which consist of other components, equipment, material, and technology that would be usable in the production of missiles and UAVs. Category II also includes, at item number 19, complete rocket systems and UAVs with a 300-km range but not capable of delivering a 500-kg payload to that range (as covered by Category I), and in item number 20, individual rocket stages and rocket engines and production equipment usable for systems with a range of 300 km with less than a 500-kg payload.

In January 1993, MTCR partners revised the guidelines to limit the risks of proliferation of missile delivery systems for all weapons of mass destruction: chemical and biological weapons as well as nuclear weapons. The guidelines now call for particular restraint and the presumption to deny transfers of any missiles (whether or not they are included in the annex) and of any items in the annex if the government judges that they are intended to be used for the delivery of weapons of mass destruction.[70] This addition is commonly referred to as a "catch-all" clause.

The MTCR has undergone a transformation from a small group of Western industrial countries to a more inclusive formal and informal group of countries. Argentina, with its Condor II missile program, was originally one of the primary targets of the regime, but that country terminated development of Condor II and is now a full partner in the MTCR. South Africa and Brazil had active missile programs but are now partners. Brazil currently chairs the MTCR. Whereas the Soviet Union was the primary source for missiles to the Third World in the 1970s and 1980s, Russia has become a partner in the MTCR. Even so, the United States has sanctioned some Russian organizations

Proliferation Control Regimes: Background and Status 47

for improper exports to Iran. China has been, and still is, another significant supplier of missiles and missile technology to developing countries, but has committed to observing the MTCR guidelines and pledged not to transfer surface-to-surface missiles that meet the MTCR thresholds. In spite of these commitments, some Russian and Chinese organizations and individuals apparently continue to supply components and technical assistance for missile production.

North Korea reportedly has become a primary supplier of missiles and missile technology to some developing countries. Iran, Syria, India, and Pakistan are the other countries of major concern regarding the development and acquisition of missiles. Missile programs in China, Egypt, and South Korea have also caused concern in Washington. Cruise missiles have always been included with ballistic missiles and space-launch vehicles in the MTCR but are now receiving greater attention as advanced propulsion and guidance technology is becoming more widely available.

The United States long ago stated its support for expanding membership of the MTCR "to include additional countries that subscribe to international non-proliferation standards, enforce effective export controls, and abandon offensive ballistic missile programs."[71] The United States will not support space launch programs in non-MTCR countries, but will consider exports of MTCR items for use in space-launch programs by MTCR countries on a case-by-case basis. The United States and other MTCR countries are promoting regional efforts to reduce the demand for missiles and persuade countries to forgo the acquisition of missiles.

Some nations have not joined the MTCR, affirming their sovereign right to acquire, develop, deploy, and export missiles. It has been particularly difficult to control dual-use technologies that may be used for civilian space launch vehicles, civil aviation, general industry, and tactical weapons.

MTCR member states have been working since about 1999 on a supplementary effort that has become known as the International Code of Conduct (ICOC) Against Ballistic Missile Proliferation. On November 25, 2002, the ICOC entered into force and the United States was an initial subscribing member. The code includes broad principles, general commitments and modest confidence-building measures. The Bush administration saw the ICOC as "an important addition to the wide range of tools available to countries to impede and roll back this proliferation threat."[72] The code attempts to fill the gap of demand-side incentives by offering "cooperation" with respect to civilian space-launch vehicle technology in exchange for significant nonproliferation commitments. However, such cooperation is to be worked out between states and is not specified in the draft document, making incentives for cooperation appear a bit elusive.

Implementing the Regime International Organization

Although the MTCR has no international organization, partner countries hold monthly meetings in Paris among embassy representatives (called "points of contact" meetings), hold technical experts' meetings (including information exchanges) and convene a plenary once each year. In this manner, partners revise the guidelines and the equipment annex and admit new partners. At the Madrid 2005 Plenary, partners emphasized that the threat of proliferation of WMD delivery systems constitutes a threat to international peace and security and stressed the need to reduce the risks associated with terrorism in this regard. This theme has been reiterated each year since.

U.S. Government Organization

The Directorate of Defense Trade Controls of the State Department administers the regulations governing the export of items on the Munitions List—those items that are subject to controls under the AECA and the ITAR.[73] The Bureau of Industry and Security in the U.S. Department of Commerce administers the regulations governing the export of items on the Commerce Control List—those items that are primarily for civilian use but have applications for the development, testing, or production of missiles.[74]

The Missile Technology Export Control (MTEC) working group is chaired by a State Department official that reviews controversial missile export license cases. The Missile Trade Analysis Group (MTAG), another interagency group chaired by a State Department representative, reviews intelligence reports on diversions of missile technology from legitimate recipients to others.[75]

Officials in the State Department's Bureau of International Security and Nonproliferation (ISN) and regional bureaus also undertake diplomatic initiatives to dissuade additional nations from developing missiles, to persuade other countries to adopt export controls on missile technology, and to reduce the perceived need for missiles.[76]

Department of Defense officials have established a counter-proliferation policy that addresses export controls, security relationships with friendly and hostile countries, defensive and offensive military operational concepts, and equipment. Many organizations within the Department implement the various aspects of the counter-proliferation policy, but the Assistant Secretary for

International Security Policy (ASD(ISP)) has the primary responsibility for counter-proliferation policy formulation.[77]

The Department of the Treasury also oversees U.S. embargoes through its Office of Foreign Assets Control (OFAC), and helps enforce export controls through the U.S. Customs Service.[78]

U.S. Laws[79]

The United States has maintained stringent controls on missiles and missile technology under the Arms Export Control Act (22 USC. 2751) and the International Traffic in Arms Regulations (22 C.F.R. Part 121, hereafter the ITAR).

In the early 1980s, the United States also unilaterally adopted tighter export controls on dual-use equipment and technology that could benefit foreign missile programs. Dual-use controls have been placed in the Export Administration Regulations (15 C.F.R. 730-799) pursuant to the authority of the Export Administration Act of 1979 (50 USC. app. 2401 et seq.) and the International Emergency Economic Powers Act (50 USC. 1701 et seq.). Successive administrations have updated regulations to reflect changes adopted by the MTCR, changes in U.S. law, and the changing international political environment. The Export Administration Act of 1979 has expired several times, but the president has invoked his authority to continue in effect the system of controls that had been maintained under the act.

Members of Congress became concerned about missile proliferation in the mid-1980s because growing evidence of missile proliferation in developing world was an additional consideration in funding President Reagan's ballistic missile defense programs. Libya had purchased Soviet Scud missiles and Iran and Iraq were firing missiles at each other. Congress had little or no involvement in shaping the MTCR, because it was neither a treaty nor an executive agreement. Soon after the regime was announced in April 1987, it became apparent that companies and individuals from a number of MTCR member countries (such as West Germany, Italy, Britain, and France) had transferred goods and technical assistance to missile development teams in Argentina, Brazil, Iraq, Egypt, and elsewhere. In 1987, the United States also learned that China had transferred intermediate range missiles to Saudi Arabia. Many Members of Congress thought the MTCR needed enforcement mechanisms, additional members, and stricter compliance.

Several bills were introduced at the time with the intention of strengthening the U.S. position on missile nonproliferation. Those bills that included sanctions against nations, companies, and individuals who violate the MTCR guidelines gained widespread bipartisan congressional support. At the time, Bush administration officials maintained that the president already had sufficient authority to reprimand or sanction foreign governments, companies, and individuals for inappropriate missile transfers and objected to the imposition of mandatory statutory sanctions. President George H.W. Bush pocket-vetoed the Export Administration Act of 1990, which included a missile nonproliferation provision, as well as the Chemical and Biological Weapons Control Act. However, he signed the defense authorization bill that contained a nearly identical section on missile nonproliferation policy.

The Missile Technology Control Act of 1990
The act became law in the 101st Congress (H.R. 4739, Title XVII of the National Defense Authorization Act for Fiscal Year 1991, P.L. 101-510). It added Chapter 7 to the Arms Export Control Act, sections 6(1) and 11B to the Export Administration Act of 1979, and established an annual reporting requirement. Chapter 7 of the AECA has been amended several times.

The Arms Export Control Act
(22 USC. 2751 et seq.) Chapter 7 of the AECA requires the president to impose sanctions on U.S. and foreign individuals who improperly conduct trade in controlled missile technology. If someone inappropriately transfers MTCR Category II goods or technology, they will be denied, for two years, any U.S. government contracts relating to missile equipment or technology, and U.S. export licenses for missile equipment and technology. The AECA requires sanctions for at least two years if a person inappropriately transfers Category I items; these include denial of all U.S. government contracts and export licenses for any item on the U.S. Munitions List. If the president determines that a foreign person has substantially contributed to the design, development, or production of missiles by a non-MTCR country, he shall prohibit for at least two years U.S. imports of items produced by that person. The act includes presidential waivers, exclusions, determination requirements, and definitions that allow the administration to take no action in certain circumstances.

These sanctions may be waived by the president, and they generally do not apply to transfers of missile goods or technology to an MTCR adherent or from an MTCR adherent. The United States has imposed missile sanctions against entities in several countries including China, Pakistan, South Africa, North Korea, Iran, Russia, India, Syria, and Egypt.

The Export Administration Act of 1979

(Sections 6 (l) and 11B, 50 USC. app. 2405 and app. 2410b). Similarly, the EAA requires controls on U.S. missile-related exports and sanctions against U.S. and foreign persons who improperly transfer dual-use goods or technology listed in the MTCR annex.

If a person improperly transfers Category II goods or technology, he will be denied export licenses for two years for missile equipment and technology controlled under the EAA. If a person improperly exports Category I goods or technology, he will be denied export licenses for at least two years for all items controlled under the EAA.

If a foreign person exports goods or technology that substantially contribute to the design, development, or production of missiles in a non-MTCR country, he will be denied license to import his products into the United States for at least two years. Actions that trigger sanctions under the provisions of either the AECA or the EAA, require commensurate sanctions under the other act.

Additional Missile Nonproliferation Policy Provisions in Legislation

Over the years, Congress has called for additional sanctions, expressed views to strengthen nonproliferation policies related to missiles or advanced conventional weapons, and expressed views on improving the organization of the U.S. government to implement those policies in several other laws. There are provisions related to missile proliferation in the Foreign Assistance Act of 1961, the Iran, North Korea and Syria Nonproliferation Act, the Iran-Iraq Arms Nonproliferation Act of 1992, the Freedom Support Act, and the Cooperative Threat Reduction Act. These and other laws are listed in *Appendix B.*

Issues for the 111th Congress

A perennial issue of varying interest is whether the MTCR and the associated U.S. sanctions are effective enough to warrant the economic and political costs to the United States, and whether additional or alternative feasible measures would increase effectiveness.

Many analysts consider the MTCR a successful vehicle for quiet diplomacy. The MTCR has been credited with slowing missile development in Brazil and India, and blocking a collaborative program of Argentina, Egypt, and Iraq to build the Condor missile.

This missile would have been a significant improvement over the Scud-based missiles used by Iraq in the Gulf War. Russia and China have probably stopped exporting entire missiles that fall under the parameters of the MTCR, even though some entities within those countries may continue to transfer components and technology.

Most European countries and Asian allies have tightened their export control laws and some have prosecuted individuals who have smuggled missile technology as well as nuclear and chemical production technology. Long-range ballistic missiles are expensive and extraordinarily difficult to develop and produce.

Because most countries cannot produce and integrate all of the sophisticated components required, many observers argue the MTCR and complementary export controls will probably continue to impede development of the most advanced missiles.

The major ongoing challenge, however, is that much of the international commerce in missiles and missile technology occurs between nations that do not adhere to MTCR guidelines. China and North Korea are not members, although China promised to observe the guidelines after the United States had twice imposed economic sanctions on Chinese companies for transferring missile items to Pakistan, on the condition that the United States would lift those sanctions.

North Korea's missile development, production, deployment, and export of missiles has continued largely outside the reach of the MTCR. Reported North Korean exports of missile production technology to Iran, Pakistan, Syria, and Egypt seriously undercut the international standards and goals of the regime.

In the view of some analysts, the activities of North Korea demonstrate the failure of the MTCR and the necessity of other measures. Other analysts argue North Korea demonstrates the need to expand the regime in order to make it even more difficult for such missile proliferation to occur.

Some difficulties associated with the nuclear, chemical, and biological nonproliferation regimes may be even more acute with respect to missile technology. The notion of a suppliers' regime dividing the world into "haves" and have-nots" is even more exacerbated in the case of missiles, because there is no treaty and no *quid pro quo* for the have-nots.

The International Code of Conduct is an attempt to address this "carrot" side of the carrot-stick equation, but the lack of specificity on incentives is viewed by some as too limited and by others as too potentially expansive. Also, there is a common perception that technology is shared among MTCR members, although the guidelines call for the strong presumption of denial of Category I-class missiles and technology to anyone.

The U.S. decision in 2002 to elaborate what constitutes "rare occasions" (wherein Category I presumption of denials could be overruled) lends credence to this view.[80]

Further, although many of the materials associated with nuclear weapons can be identified and controlled, the materials and components used in missiles are commonly used in a wide range of commercial manufacturing processes. Ballistic missile programs can be nearly indistinguishable from civilian space launch programs, and some missile production equipment, technology, and materials are difficult to distinguish from civilian items. This is particularly acute in the case of UAVs.

As some developing nations become increasingly capable of producing missiles indigenously, the effectiveness of supplier controls may gradually erode. Some analysts see attempts to control missile technology exports as futile and argue for the fewest export restrictions possible, emphasizing the importance to the U.S. economy of exports.

Others say the U.S. government should not allow the export of any goods that are likely to harm U.S. national security, despite the potential positive effect on some American business interests.

In addition to the promotion of exports, other foreign policy and national security goals may also compete with missile nonproliferation for government attention and action. For instance, U.S. leaders hope to encourage Russia and China to become stable and responsible actors in their regions and in the international community, to pursue economic and political reforms, and to respect internationally recognized human rights.

The United States has sought the cooperation of those two countries and many others in efforts to block nuclear proliferation, terrorism, drug trafficking, and organized crime. Although missile nonproliferation will remain an issue of utmost importance, other goals may occasionally be given greater emphasis.

However, when political leaders suspend missile nonproliferation policies in favor of other goals, the credibility of the U.S. policy and that of the MTCR can be damaged, according to many observers. It can become more difficult to persuade other countries to comply with a set of standards when the United

States appears to enforce the standards on a selective basis. The priority to be given to missile nonproliferation was occasionally a point of contention between Congress and the Bush administration.

Congress has established economic sanctions that must be imposed on companies that trade in missile technology contrary to the MTCR guidelines. The imposition, lifting, and waiving of these sanctions frequently cause controversy.

Some analysts suggest these negative actions should be coupled with positive incentives to induce countries to refrain from proliferation. Positive incentives could include trade credits, development assistance, military assistance, technology transfers, access to space launch and satellite capabilities, or security guaranties. But other analysts contend the security benefits derived from adhering to the MTCR should be sufficient and that the United States should not try to buy compliance.

According to many foreign policy specialists, the underlying political and security problems that drive proliferation must be resolved before meaningful curbs can be applied to the spread of weapons of mass destruction and missiles.

The United States and its partners in the MTCR have helped countries, particularly neighbors in regions of ongoing conflict, adopt confidence-building measures such as those that have contributed to security and cooperation in Europe. Many of these same countries also try to help correct regional imbalances of military forces and to facilitate peace negotiations and arms control talks.

Security alliances and military assistance also can play a role in restraining missile development. The U.S. security umbrella over Western Europe and parts of Asia and the transfer of large quantities of advanced conventional weapons helped dissuade a number of U.S. allies from developing weapons of mass destruction and helped deter aggression.

Some analysts contend that the security of some allies was enhanced by the deterrent power of U.S. nuclear-armed missiles previously deployed in their territory or, possibly in the case of Israel, by indigenous weapons. The U.S. government has also decided that it is appropriate to sell missiles (U.S. Army Tactical Missile Systems) with a potential range of 250 km to countries such as Turkey, Greece, South Korea, Britain, France, and Germany, though it forbids sales of missiles with a range of more than 300 km. However, the superiority of U.S. military technology may actually persuade some adversary countries to develop weapons of mass destruction and missiles as their best means of deterring U.S. intervention.

Some analysts see missile defense systems as a proper alternative to export controls, though most see them as supplementing other military, political, and long-range economic measures (including export controls and sanctions).

The United States will likely continue to deploy theater and long-range missile defense systems and has provided such defensive missiles and capabilities to friends and allies in Europe, East Asia, and the Middle East.

As the United States seeks to increase defense cooperation in the area of missile defenses, a few have raised issues over the applicability of MTCR guidelines. Additionally, as longer range ballistic missile defense systems are developed, some might question the transfer of such systems or technologies to other countries in the context of the MTCR. For instance, would Chinese development of intermediate-range ballistic missile defense systems be widely viewed as a permitted MTCR export to countries such as Pakistan?

Air defense missiles and anti-theater ballistic missiles probably enhance the security of U.S. allies, but none are expected to be 100% effective. In some cases, such as Taiwan, deployments might increase tensions. The Obama administration and Congress will likely continue to review defense and missile nonproliferation policy objectives in this area.

APPENDIX A. PROLIFERATION CONTROL REGIME MEMBERSHIP

NSG (45)	MTCR (34)	Australia Group (41)
Argentinaa	Argentina	Argentina
Australiaa	Australia	Australia
Austriaa	Austria	Austria
Belarus		
Belgiuma	Belgium	Belgium
Brazil	Brazil	
Bulgariaa	Bulgaria	Bulgaria
Canadaa	Canada	Canada
Chinaa		
Croatia		Croatia
Cyprusa		Cyprus
Czech Republica	Czech Republic	Czech Republic

Appendix A. (Continued)

NSG (45)	MTCR (34)	Australia Group (41)
Denmarka	Denmark	Denmark
Estonia		Estonia
		European Commission
Finlanda	Finland	Finland
Francea	France	France
Germanya	Germany	Germany
Greecea	Greece	Greece
Hungarya	Hungary	Hungary
	Iceland	Iceland
Irelanda	Ireland	Ireland
Italya	Italy	Italy
Japana	Japan	Japan
Kazakhstana		
Latvia		Latvia
Lithuania		Lithuania
Luxembourga	Luxembourg	Luxembourg
Malta		Malta
Netherlandsa	Netherlands	Netherlands
New Zealand	New Zealand	New Zealand
Norwaya	Norway	Norway
Polanda	Poland	Poland
Portugala	Portugal	Portugal
Romaniaa		Romania
Russian Federationa	Russian Federation	
Slovakiaa		Slovakia
Sloveniaa		Slovenia
South Africaa	South Africa	
South Koreaa	South Korea	South Korea
SpainaSwedena	Spain Sweden	Spain Sweden
Switzerlanda	Switzerland	Switzerland
TurkeyaUkrainea	Turkey Ukraine	Turkey Ukraine
United Kingdoma United Statesa	United Kingdom United States	United Kingdom United States

APPENDIX B. ADDITIONAL LEGISLATION AND EXECUTIVE ORDERS

Combating Proliferation of Weapons of Mass Destruction Act of 1996, Title VII, Intelligence Authorization Act for Fiscal Year 1997, P.L. 104-293, 50 USC. 2301 note.

National Defense Authorization Act for Fiscal Year 1994, Title XVI, Arms Control Matters, Nonproliferation Provisions, P.L. 103-160.

National Defense Authorization Act for Fiscal Year 1995, Title XV, Arms Control Matters, Nonproliferation Provisions, P.L. 103-337; 22 USC. 2751 note.

Weapons of Mass Destruction Control Act of 1992, Title XV, National Defense Authorization Act for Fiscal Year 1993, P.L. 102-484; 22 USC. 5859a begins at section 1505 of Act.

Antiterrorism and Effective Death Penalty Act of 1996, Title V, Nuclear, Biological, and Chemical Weapons Restrictions, P.L. 104-132, 18 USC. 831 note, and 2331, 42 USC. 262 note, 50 USC. 1522 note.

Arms Control and Nonproliferation Act of 1994, Title VIII, Part A, Foreign Relations Authorization Act, Fiscal Years 1994 and 1995, P.L. 103-236, 22 USC. 2551 note.

Defense Against Weapons of Mass Destruction Act of 1996, Title XIV, National Defense Authorization Act for Fiscal Year 1997, P.L. 104-201, 50 USC. 2301 note.

Foreign Relations Authorization Act, Fiscal Year 2003, Title XI and XIII: Verification of Arms Control and Nonproliferation Agreements, Assistance - P.L. 107-228 (Sec. 1101) 22 USC 2651 note.

Executive Order 13382 (June 28, 2005, 70 FR 38567) Blocking Property of Weapons of Mass Destruction Proliferators and Their Supporters.

Executive Order 13222 (August 17, 2001, 66 FR 44025, August 22, 2001) Continuation of Export Control Regulations, upon the expiration of the Export Administration Act of 1979.

Continued on August 15, 2002 by notice published in Federal Register on August 16, 2002.

Executive Order 13128 (June 25, 1999, 99FR 16634) Implementation of the Chemical Weapons Convention and the Chemical Weapons Convention Implementation Act.

Executive Order 13049 (June 11, 1997, 62 FR 32471) Organization for the Prohibition of Chemical Weapons.

Executive Order 13030 (December 12, 1996, 61 FR 66187) Administration of Foreign Assistance and Arms Exports.

Executive Order 12938 (November 14, 1994, 59 F.R. 59-9, 50 USC. 1701 note) Declares the proliferation of weapons of mass destruction and their means of delivery as an unusual and extraordinary threat and declares a national emergency to deal with that threat. *Amended by EO 13094 (July 28, 1998, 63 FR40803 and by EO 13128 (June 25, 1999, 64 FR 34703).*

Executive Order 12946 (January 20, 1995, 60 F.R. 4829, 22 USC. 2551 note) Establishes the president's Advisory Board on Arms Proliferation Policy.

Executive Order 12851 (June 11, 1993, 58 F.R. 33181, 22 USC. 2797 note) Delegates president's authority under the Export Administration Act, Arms Control Export Act, and the Chemical and Biological Weapons Control, Warfare Elimination Act, National Defense Authorization Act for Fiscal Years 1992 and 1993, National Defense Authorization Act for Fiscal Year 1993, and Foreign Relations Authorizations Act for Fiscal Years 1992 and 1993, to the Secretaries of State, Commerce, Defense, and Treasury, and Director of ACDA.

Executive Order 11850 (April 8, 1975, 40 F.R. 16187, 50 USC. 1511 note) Renunciation of certain uses in war of chemical herbicides and riot control agents.

End Notes

[1] See also CRS Report RL33865, Arms Control and Nonproliferation: A Catalog of Treaties and Agreements, by Amy F. Woolf, Mary Beth Nikitin, and Paul K. Kerr.

[2] See CRS Report RL34327, Proliferation Security Initiative (PSI), by Mary Beth Nikitin.

[3] For a current summary, see CRS Report RL30699, Nuclear, Biological, and Chemical Weapons and Missiles: Status and Trends, by Paul K. Kerr.

[4] For details, see "South Africa Profile: Nuclear Overview," Nuclear Threat Initiative website, http://www.nti.org/ e_research/profiles/SAfrica/Nuclear/index_2153.html.

[5] See CRS Report RS21823, Disarming Libya: Weapons of Mass Destruction, by Sharon Squassoni.

[6] Previous proposals included a 1945 proposal by the United States, Britain, and Canada proposed to establish a U.N. Atomic Energy Commission to eliminate "the use of atomic energy for destructive purposes," a 1957 "package" of measures (from Canada, UK, France, and United States) to the U.N. Disarmament Commission that included a commitment not to transfer nuclear weapons, a 1964 program proposed by the United States for nonproliferation. See Arms Control and Disarmament Agreements: Texts and Histories of the Negotiations, 1990 edition, U.S. Arms Control and Disarmament Agency, p. 89.

Proliferation Control Regimes: Background and Status 59

[7] This number excludes North Korea (the DPRK). North Korea announced its withdrawal from the NPT effective January 11, 2003, but no official agreement has been reached on its status amongst the NPT states parties or depositary states.

[8] These agreements are called "full-scope safeguards." Other states have partial safeguards agreements, including India, Pakistan and Israel, which can either apply to material or facilities. All of the five nuclear weapons states have voluntary safeguards agreements, which cover a portion of facilities and materials.

[9] NPT, Article IV-2.

[10] NPT, Article VI.

[11] http://www.iaea.org/Publications/Documents/Conventions/cppnm.html.

[12] See CRS Report RL33548, Comprehensive Nuclear-Test-Ban Treaty: Background and Current Developments, by Jonathan Medalia.

[13] Mohamed ElBaradei, "Rethinking Nuclear Safeguards," Washington Post, June 14, 2006.

[14] Henry Kissinger, Sam Nunn, William Perry and George Shultz, "A World Free of Nuclear Weapons," Wall Street Journal, January 4, 2007. http://www.nuclearsecurityproject. org/site/c.mjJXJbMMIoE/b.3483737/k.4057/ Nuclear_Security_Project_Home.htm

[15] http://www.whitehouse.gov/agenda/homeland_security/.

[16] See http://www.opanal.org/index-i.html.

[17] For the 2009 G8 Summit documentation see the Italian Presidency's website: http:// www. g8italia2009.it/G8/Home/ G8-G8_Layout_locale-1199882116809_Atti.htm

[18] "U.S.-Russia Joint Fact Sheet on The Global Initiative to Combat Nuclear Terrorism," July 15, 2006. Available at http://www.state.gov/r/pa/prs/ps/2006/69016.htm.

[19] http://www.whitehouse.gov/news/releases/2006/07/20060715-3.html.

[20] http://www.state.gov/t/isn/rls/fs/125325.htm

[21] For a detailed discussion, see CRS Report RL34327, Proliferation Security Initiative (PSI), by Mary Beth Nikitin.

[22] "The Agenda: Homeland Security," White House website, http://www.whitehouse. gov/agenda/homeland_security/

[23] The IAEA Statute is found at http://www.iaea.org/About/statute.html.

[24] See http://www.iaea.org/About/index.html.

[25] See GC(50)/RES/11.

[26] See GOV/2007/43-GC(51)/15.

[27] IAEA Director General Mohamed ElBaradei, "Seven Steps to Raise World Security," Financial Times, February 2, 2005.

[28] See http://www.zanggercommittee.org/Zangger/default.htm for Zangger website.

[29] See Appendix A for list of Zangger Committee members. http://www.zangger committee. org/Zangger/default.htm.

[30] See http://www.nuclearsuppliersgroup.org for NSG website.

[31] The new guidelines appeared as an International Atomic Energy Agency document, INFCIRC/254/Rev.1/Part 1 and Part 2, July 1992.

[32] See Appendix A for NSG membership.

[33] See CRS Report RL33016, U.S. Nuclear Cooperation with India: Issues for Congress, by Paul K. Kerr.

[34] An October 2007 GAO Report raises important questions about U.S. efforts to combat proliferation networks. See U.S. General Accounting Office, "U.S. Efforts to Combat Nuclear Networks Need Better Data on Proliferation Risks and Program Results," October 31, 2007. http://www.gao.gov/new.items/d0821.pdf.

[35] http://www.whitehouse.gov/agenda/homeland_security/

[36] "National Strategy to Combat Weapons of Mass Destruction," December 11, 2002. See http://www.whitehouse.gov/ news/releases/2002/12/WMDStrategy.pdf.

[37] This section drawn from CRS Report RL31502, Nuclear, Biological, Chemical, and Missile Proliferation Sanctions: Selected Current Law, by Dianne E. Rennack.

[38] P.L. 83-703, 42 USC. 2011.

[39] P.L. 95-242, 22 USC. 3201.

[40] P.L. 90-629, 22 USC. 2751. Title 22 of the U.S. Code, Chapter 39, addresses Arms Export Control. Subchapter VII addresses control of missiles and missile exports or technology; subchapter VIII addresses chemical weapons and biological weapons, and subchapter X addresses nuclear nonproliferation controls.

[41] See CRS Report RL31832, The Export Administration Act: Evolution, Provisions, and Debate, by Ian F. Fergusson.

[42] See The Export-Import Bank Reauthorization Act of 2002, P.L. 107-189.

[43] See CRS Report 97-1027, Nunn-Lugar Cooperative Threat Reduction Programs: Issues for Congress, by Amy F. Woolf.

[44] See CRS Report RL31957, Nonproliferation and Threat Reduction Assistance: U.S. Programs in the Former Soviet Union, by Amy F. Woolf

[45] This section was prepared by Paul Kerr.

[46] United Nations Institute for Disarmament Research, "Blood, Toil, Tears and Sweat: The Biological and Toxin Weapons Convention since 2001," Disarmament Forum, 2006.

[47] http://www.opcw.org.

[48] For more information about the CWC's status, see CRS Report RL 33865, Arms Control and Nonproliferation: A Catalog of Treaties and Agreements, by Amy F. Woolf, Mary Beth Nikitin, and Paul K Kerr.

[49] http://www.fas.org/nuke/control/bwc/text/bwc.htm.

[50] For more information about the BWC's status, see CRS Report RL 33865.

[51] http://www.unog.ch/80256EE600585943/ (httpPages)/16C37624830EDAE5 C12572BC0044 DFC1?OpenDocument.

[52] By virtue of the treaty-prescribed method of selecting rotational members, the United States will always have a seat on the Executive Council.

[53] This section drawn from CRS Report RL31502, Nuclear, Biological, Chemical, and Missile Proliferation Sanctions: Selected Current Law, by Dianne E. Rennack.

[54] Title III, P.L. 102-182, 22 USC. 5601-5606.

[55] Taken from CRS Report RL 31832, The Export Administration Act: Evolution, Provisions, and Debate, by Ian F. Fergusson. See that report for more information on the proposed legislation.

[56] Ambassador Eric Javits, U.S. Permanent Representative to the OPCW, Statement Concerning Request to Extend the United States' Destruction Deadline Under the Chemical Weapons Convention, April 20, 2006. Available at http://www.state.gov/t/isn/rls/rm/64878.htm.

[57] Ibid.

[58] The United States has destroyed all of its chemical weapons munitions.

[59] These sites are managed by the U.S. Army Chemical Materials Agency (CMA). The facilities under construction in Colorado and Kentucky are managed by the Assembled Chemical Weapons Alternatives program.

[60] Department of Defense Report Chemical Demilitarization Program Semi-Annual Report to Congress, May 2009.

[61] See ACWA Cost and Schedule Information. Available at http://www.pmacwa.army.mil/ip/dl/ acwa_cost_schedule.pdf

Proliferation Control Regimes: Background and Status 61

[62] Chemical Demilitarization Program Semi-Annual Report to Congress, 2008.

[63] In section 923 of P.L. 109-364.

[64] Chemical Demilitarization Program Semi-Annual Report to Congress, 2009.

[65] Analyst interview with ACWA official, January 28, 2010.

[66] Decision Programme and Budget of the OPCW for 2010, December 2, 2009, C-14/DEC.8.

[67] CRS Report RL32891, The National Biodefense Analysis and Countermeasures Center: Issues for Congress, by Dana A. Shea. See also, Jonathan Tucker, "Seeking Biosecurity Without Verification: The New U.S. Strategy on Biothreats," Arms Control Today, January/February 2010.

[68] This section was prepared by Steven A. Hildreth.

[69] See Appendix A for a list of current partners.

[70] According to the guidelines, the government judgment on the likely use of the missile items will be made, "on the basis of all available, persuasive information, evaluated according to factors including:

A. Concerns about the proliferation of weapons of mass destruction;

B. The capabilities and objectives of the missile and space programs of the recipient

C. The significance of the transfer in terms of the potential development of delivery systems (other than manned aircraft) for weapons of mass destruction;

D. The assessment of the end-use of the transfers, including the relevant assurances of the recipient states ... ; and

E. The applicability of relevant multilateral agreements."

[71] U.S. Department of State, Reprint of White House Press Release, Non-Proliferation and Export Control Policy, September 27, 1993.

[72] John R. Bolton, Remarks at the Launching Conference for the ICOC, The Hague, The Netherlands, November 25, 2002. See http://www.state.gov/t/us/rm/15488.htm.

[73] http://www.pmddtc.state.gov

[74] http://www.bis.doc.gov

[75] http://www.state.gov/t/isn/58386.htm

[76] http://www.state.gov/t/isn

[77] http://www.fas.org/irp/doddir/dod/ds111_14.pdf

[78] http://www.treas.gov.offices/enforcement/ofac

[79] This section drawn from CRS Report RL31502, Nuclear, Biological, Chemical, and Missile Proliferation Sanctions: Selected Current Law, by Dianne E. Rennack.

[80] Testimony given by Vann Van Diepen, Deputy Assistant Secretary of State for Proliferation Controls in a hearing before Senate Government Affairs Committee, Subcommittee on International Security, Proliferation and Federal Services, June 11, 2002

In: Proliferation Security Measures
Editors: R. Cooke & E. Velazquez

ISBN: 978-1-62081-014-9
© 2012 Nova Science Publishers, Inc

Chapter 2

NUCLEAR, BIOLOGICAL, CHEMICAL, AND MISSILE PROLIFERATION SANCTIONS: SELECTED CURRENT LAW[*]

Dianne E. Rennack

SUMMARY

The proliferation of nuclear, biological, and chemical weapons, and the means to deliver them, are front and center today for policy makers who guide and form U.S. foreign policy and national security policy, and economic sanctions are considered a valuable asset in the national security and foreign policy toolbox. The United States currently maintains robust sanctions regimes against foreign governments it has identified as proliferators (particularly Iran, North Korea, and Syria). If the 112th Congress takes up even a fraction of the proposals introduced by its predecessor involving economic sanctions, the president and the Departments of State, Commerce, and Treasury—those agencies that implement and administer the bulk of sanctions regimes—will likely find the role of Congress in determining the use of sanctions also robust.

This report offers a listing and brief description of legal provisions that require or authorize the imposition of some form of economic sanction against countries, companies, persons, or entities that violate

---

[*] This is an edited, reformatted and augmented version of a Congressional Research Service publication, CRS Report for Congress RL31502, from www.crs.gov, prepared for Members and Committees of Congress, dated November 30, 2010.

U.S. nonproliferation norms. For each provision, information is included on what triggers the imposition of sanctions, their duration, what authority the president has to delay or abstain from imposing sanctions, and what authority the president has to waive the imposition of sanctions.

BACKGROUND

The use of economic sanctions to stem weapons proliferation acquired a new dimension in the 1990s.[1] While earlier legislation required the cutoff of foreign aid to countries engaged in specified nuclear proliferation activities and mentioned other sanctions as a possible mechanism for bringing countries into compliance with goals of treaties or international agreements,[2] it was not until 1990 that Congress enacted explicit guidelines for trade sanctions related to missile proliferation. In that year a requirement for the president to impose sanctions against U.S. persons or foreign persons engaging in trade of items or technology listed in the Missile Technology Control Regime Annex (MTCR Annex) was added to the Arms Export Control Act and to the Export Administration Act of 1979. Subsequently, Congress legislated economic sanctions against countries that contribute to the proliferation of chemical, biological, and nuclear weapons in a broad array of laws.

The use of economic sanctions in furtherance of foreign policy or national security policy fell into disfavor in the mid- to late 1990s, in reaction to reports of the substantial toll paid by civilian populations when sanctions were cast broadly or wielded as a blunt force. At the same time, however, concerns about nuclear weapons proliferation shifted into high gear, fueled by nuclear weapons tests conducted by India and Pakistan (1998), and later by North Korea (2006 and 2009), North Korea's formal withdrawal from the Nuclear Nonproliferation Treaty (2003), multiple missile tests by North Korea, reports of Iraq having weapons of mass production, possibly chemical and biological (leading into war in 2003); Iran's noncompliance with international agreements (which the International Atomic Energy Act began reporting in 2005), and the 2004 discovery that a leading nuclear scientist in Pakistan—A.Q. Khan—had been selling nuclear materials, technology, and knowledge to the highest bidder, including North Korea, Iraq, Iran, and Libya, for more than a decade.

The 111th Congress enacted the Comprehensive Iran Sanctions, Accountability, and Divestment Act of 2010, but some have expressed concern that the executive branch is taking full advantage of flexibility the Act provides in its implementation. The new Congress might revisit this legislation. Unfinished initiatives of the 111th Congress raise the possibility that Belarus, Burma, Pakistan, Saudi Arabia, the United Arab Emirates, and Venezuela are supporting proliferation of weapons of mass destruction. Events of recent weeks signaling North Korea's and Iran's belligerence, disclosure of classified diplomatic documents that has churned up speculation and conjecture in the policy making and policy analysis communities, and the shift in political power particularly in the House of Representatives, could all have an impact on the 112th Congress's approach to both sanctions and proliferation concerns. Other foreign policy and national security concerns—terrorism, regional stability, human rights, and the nexus among these issues that shape rogue regimes—could result in increased use of economic sanctions.

President Obama has also initiated a scrutiny of U.S. export policy, with an eye toward streamlining licensing procedures and increasing exports. Many statutes that establish an authority or a requirement to impose economic sanctions to deter proliferation are implicated in export controls and thus are likely to be at least impacted by export control reforms, and perhaps will present an obstacle to that reform.

This report offers an alphabetic listing and brief description of legal provisions that require or authorize the imposition of some form of economic sanction on countries, companies, or persons who violate U.S. nonproliferation norms.[3] For each provision, information is included on what triggers the imposition of sanctions, their duration, what authority the president has to delay or abstain from imposing sanctions, and what authority the president has to waive the imposition of sanctions.

SELECTED CURRENT LAW: SANCTIONS PROVISIONS

18 USC. (Relating to Criminal Procedure)

18 USC. 229-229F (part I, chapter 11) makes it generally unlawful for a person knowingly "(1) to develop, produce, otherwise acquire, transfer directly or indirectly, receive, stockpile, retain, own, possess, or use, or threaten to use, any chemical weapon; or (2) to assist, induce, in any way, any person to violate paragraph (1), or to attempt or conspire to violate paragraph (1)." The sections establish criminal and civil penalties, and terms of criminal forfeiture.

Sec. 201 of the Chemical Weapons Convention Implementation Act of 1998 (Division I of P.L. 105-277; approved October 21, 1998) enacted these sections to bring the criminal and civil penalties section of United States Code into conformity with the requirements of the Chemical Weapons Convention. Sec. 211 of that Act, furthermore, authorized the president to suspend or revoke export privileges of anyone found in violation of 18 USC. 229. P.L. 109-304 (enacted Oct. 6, 2006) made a technical correction.

18 USC. 832 makes it an offense to attempt to willfully participate in or knowingly provide material support or resources to a nuclear weapons program or other weapons of mass destruction (WMD) program of a foreign terrorist power. Such an offense is punishable by imprisonment of not more than 20 years. The section also makes it an offense to develop, possess, or attempt or conspire to develop or possess, a radiological weapon, to threaten to use, or use, such a weapon against any person in the United States, and any U.S. national regardless of where he/she may be, or against property owned or used by the United States. Such offense is punishable by imprisonment for "any term of years or for life."

Sec. 6803(c) of the Weapons of Mass Destruction Prohibition Improvement Act of 2004 (title VI, subtitle I, of the Intelligence Reform and Terrorism Prevention Act of 2004; P.L. 108-458; approved December 17, 2004) added sec. 832.

18 USC. 2332a makes it an offense to use, threaten to use, attempt or conspire to use WMD against a national of the United States or within the United States. A "weapon of mass destruction" is a destructive device as defined in 18 USC. 921—any explosive, incendiary, or poison gas bomb, grenade, mine, or rocket or missile of a certain size, any type of weapon of a certain size that delivers its projectile by explosion or other propellant—and any weapon that delivers toxic or poisonous chemicals, biological agent, toxin, or vector, radiation, or radioactivity. One found to have used a WMD "shall be imprisoned for any term of years or for life, and if death results, shall be punished by death or imprisoned for any term of years or for life."

Sec. 60023(a) of P.L. 103-322 (108 Stat. 1980) added sec. 2332a. The section was substantially reworked by the Antiterrorism and Effective Death Penalty Act of 1996 (P.L. 104-132; approved April 24, 1996). The Chemical Weapons Convention Implementation Act of 1998 (division I of P.L. 105-277; approved October 21, 1998) exempted chemical weapons from application of this section of 18 USC., and in its place enacted chapter 11B of part I of 18 USC. (secs. 229 through 229F, above) to establish criminal and civil penalties in conformity with the Chemical Weapons Convention. The Economic Espionage Act of 1996(P.L. 104-294; approved October 11, 1996) and the Public Health Security and Bioterrorism Preparedness and Response Act of

2002 (P.L. 107-188; approved June 12, 2002) made technical changes. The Weapons of Mass Destruction Prohibition Improvement Act of 2004 (title VI, subtitle I, of the Intelligence Reform and Terrorism Prevention Act of 2004; P.L. 108-458; approved December 17, 2004) expanded the means of delivering the WMD to include the U.S. mail service and variations on "foreign commerce," included attacks against property, and changed the section heading from "Use of certain weapons of mass destruction" to "Use of weapons of mass destruction," consolidating WMD-related offenses in this chapter and section.

Arms Export Control Act[4]

The Arms Export Control Act (AECA), as amended, authorizes U.S. government military sales, loans, leases, and financing, and licensing of commercial arms sales to other countries. The AECA requires the president to coordinate such actions with other foreign policy considerations, including nonproliferation, and states guidelines by which the president determines eligibility of recipients for military exports, sales, leases, loans, and financing.

Section 3(f) (Eligibility; 22 USC. 2753(f)) prohibits U.S. military sales or leases to any country that the president determines is in material breach of binding commitments to the United States under international treaties or agreements regarding nonproliferation of nuclear explosive devices and unsafeguarded special nuclear material.

Subsec. (f) was added by sec. 822(a)(1) of the Nuclear Proliferation Prevention Act of 1994 (title VIII of the Foreign Relations Authorization Act, Fiscal Years 1994 and 1995; P.L. 103-236; approved April 30, 1994).

Section 38 (Control of Arms Exports and Imports; 22 USC. 2778) authorizes the president, "in furtherance of world peace and the security and foreign policy of the United States," to control the import and export of defense articles and services, to provide foreign policy guidelines to U.S. importers/exporters, and to promulgate the United States Munitions List (USML) constituting what defense articles and services are regulated. Section 38(c) establishes that any person who willfully violates any provision of the section, section 39 (relating to the reporting of fees, contributions, gifts, and commissions paid by those involved in commercial sales of defense articles or services), certain treaties, or rules and regulations relating to any of these provisions, may be fined not more than $1 million (for each violation), imprisoned not more than 20 years, or both. Section 38(e) authorizes the

Secretary of State to assess civil penalties and initiate civil actions against violators; any civil penalty for violations under this section is capped at $500,000. Section 38(j) authorizes the president to exempt a foreign country from licensing requirements under the AECA when that country commits to a binding bilateral agreement with the United States to establish export controls on a par with export controls in U.S. law and regulations, or in instances where particular defense trade cooperation treaties are a factor.

Section 38 was added by sec. 212(a)(1) of the International Security Assistance and Arms Export Control Act of 1976 (P.L. 94-329; approved June 30, 1976). Subsec. (c) was added by the 1976 amendment; the fine and imprisonment terms were amended, however, by sec. 119(a) of the International Security and Development Cooperation Act of 1985 (P.L. 99-83; approved August 8, 1985). Formerly, fine was "not more than $100,000," and period of imprisonment was not more than two years. Sec. 107(a)(2) of the Comprehensive Iran Sanctions, Accountability, and Divestment Act of 2010 (P.L. 111-195; approved July 10, 2010) extended the imprisonment terms from 10 years to twenty. Applicability of subsecs. (c), (e), (f), and (j) were expanded to include certain defense treaties by sec.103(a) of the Defense Trade Cooperation Treaties Implementation Act of 2010 (title I of the Security Cooperation Act of 2010; P.L. 111-266; approved October 8, 2010). Subsec. (e) was added by the 1976 amendment. Sec. 119(b) of P.L. 99-83, in 1985, however, added the language that caps civil penalties, and sec. 1303 of the Arms Control, Nonproliferation and Security Assistance Act of 1999 (division B of the Nance/Donovan Foreign Relations Authorization Act, FY 2000-2001; H.R. 3427, enacted by reference in P.L. 106-113), gave civil action authority to the Secretary of State. Previously the section referred to such authority in the Export Administration Act, which resides with the Secretary of Commerce and was capped in that Act at $100,000.Sec. 102(a) of the Security Assistance Act of 2000 (P.L. 106- 280; approved October 6, 2000) limited the president's authority to exempt a foreign country from certain licensing exceptions in subsec. (f), and added subsec. (j). Sec. 6910 of the Prevention of Terrorist Access to Destructive Weapons Act of 2004 (subtitle J, title VI, of the Intelligence Reform and Terrorism Prevention Act of 2004; P.L. 108-458; 118 Stat. 3774) expanded requirements on the president to develop mechanisms to identify persons subject to various Public Laws that restrict transactions related to WMD.

Section 40 (Transactions With Countries Supporting Acts of International Terrorism; 22 USC. 2780) prohibits exporting or otherwise providing munitions, providing financial assistance to facilitate transfer of munitions,

Nuclear, Biological, Chemical, and Missile Proliferation Sanctions 69

granting eligibility to such transfers, issuing licenses for such transfers, or facilitating the acquisition of munitions to a country the government of which "has repeatedly provided support for acts of international terrorism." The section includes in its definition of acts of international terrorism, "all activities that the Secretary [of State] determines willfully aid or abet the international proliferation of nuclear explosive devices to individuals or groups, willfully aid or abet an individual or groups in acquiring unsafeguarded special nuclear material, or willfully aid or abet the efforts of an individual or group to use, development, produce, stockpile, or otherwise acquire chemical, biological, or radiological weapons."

The president may rescind the Secretary's determination (sec. 40(f)) by reporting to the Speaker of the House and the Chairperson of the Senate Foreign Relations Committee, before issuing the rescission, that the leadership and policies of the country in question have changed, the government is not supporting international terrorism, and the government has issued assurances that it will not support international terrorism in the future. Congress may block the rescission of the terrorist determination by enacting a joint resolution. The president, however, may unilaterally waive any or all of the prohibitions in this section if he determines to do so is essential to the national security interests of the United States, and so reports to Congress.

Those found to be in violation of the section face criminal prosecution with penalties of as much as a $1 million fine and imprisonment of not more than 20 years. Civil penalties for violations under this section, similar to those in sec. 38, are capped at $500,000; the Secretary of State has the authority to assess civil penalties and initiate civil actions against violators.

Section 40 was added by the Omnibus Diplomatic Security and Antiterrorism Act of 1986 (P.L. 99-399; approved August 27, 1986), and later amended and restated by the Anti-Terrorism and Arms Export Amendments Act of 1989 (P.L. 101-222; approved August 27, 1986). Sec. 822(a)(2)(A) of the Nuclear Proliferation Prevention Act of 1994 (title VIII of the Foreign Relations Authorization Act, Fiscal Years 1994 and 1995; P.L. 103-236; approved April 30, 1994) added a definition of acts of international terrorism that would lead the Secretary of State to make a determination. The same section added definitions "nuclear explosive device" and "unsafeguarded special nuclear material." Sec. 321 of the Foreign Relations Authorization Act, Fiscal Years 1992 and 1993 (P.L. 102-138; approved October 28, 1991), made technical changes to the guidelines for Congress's passage of a joint resolution relating to the section. Sec. 1303 of the Arms Control, Nonproliferation and Security Assistance Act of 1999 (division B of the

Nance/Donovan Foreign Relations Authorization Act, FY 2000-2001; H.R. 3427, enacted by reference in P.L. 106-113) gave civil action authority to the Secretary of State. Previously the section referred to such authority in the Export Administration Act, which resides with the Secretary of Commerce and was capped in that Act at $100,000. Sec. 1204 of the Foreign Relations Authorization Act, Fiscal Year 2003 (P.L. 107-228; approved September 30, 2002), expanded the definitions to make the sanctions applicable to an individual or group in pursuit of chemical, biological, or radiological weapons. Sec. 107(a)(3) of the Comprehensive Iran Sanctions, Accountability, and Divestment Act of 2010 (P.L. 111-195; approved July 10, 2010) extended the imprisonment terms from 10 years to twenty.

Sections 72 and 73 (Denial of the Transfer of Missile Equipment or Technology by U.S. Persons; 22 USC. 2797a; Transfers of Missile Equipment or Technology by Foreign Persons; 2797b), require sanctions against any U.S. citizen or any foreign person whom the president determines to be engaged in exporting, transferring, conspiring to export or transfer, or facilitating an export or transfer of, any equipment or technology identified by the Missile Technology Control Regime (MTCR) that "contributes to the acquisition, design, development, or production of missiles in a country that is not an MTCR adherent...."

Sanctions vary with the type of equipment or technology exported, and are increasingly severe where the type of equipment or technology is more controlled. Worst-case sanctions may be imposed for not less than two years, and include denial of U.S. government contracts, denial of export licenses for items on the U.S. Munitions List, and a prohibition on importation into the United States.

The law allows several exceptions, wherein some or all of the sanctions may not be imposed against foreign persons:

- if an MTCR adherent with jurisdictional authority finds the foreign person innocent of wrongdoing in relation to the transaction;
- if the State Department issues an advisory opinion to the individual stating that a transaction would not result in sanctions;
- if the export, transfer, or trading activity is authorized by the laws of an MTCR adherent and not obtained by misrepresentation or fraud, except when the activity in question is conducted by an entity subordinate to a government of an independent state of the former Soviet Union, and when the president determines that government has

Nuclear, Biological, Chemical, and Missile Proliferation Sanctions   71

knowingly transferred missiles or missile technology in a manner inconsistent with MTCR guidelines;

- if the export, transfer, or trade is made to an end-user in a country that is an MTCR adherent;
- in the case of foreign persons fulfilling contracts for defense services or defense articles; then the president will not prohibit importations if
  - the articles or services are considered essential to U.S. national security,
  - the president determines that the provider is a sole supplier and the articles or services are essential to U.S. national security, or
  - the president determines that the articles or services are essential to U.S. national security under defense cooperation agreements or NATO Programs of Cooperation;
- in the case of foreign persons importing products or services into the United States in fulfillment of contracts entered into before the president announces intentions to impose sanctions, then the president will not prohibit importations; or
- in the case of foreign persons providing spare parts, component parts essential to U.S. products or production, routine service and maintenance, essential information and technology.

Sanctions are not imposed, or those imposed may be lifted, against individuals when the president certifies that a foreign government, which is an MTCR adherent, has adequately attended to the violation through some judicial process or enforcement action.

The president may waive the sanction, for either a U.S. citizen or foreign person, if he certifies to Congress that it is essential to the national security of the United States, or that the individual provides a product or service essential to U.S. national security, and that person is a sole source provider of the product or service.

Section 1703 of the National Defense Authorization Act for Fiscal Year 1991 (P.L. 101-510; approved November 5, 1990) added sections 71-74. In section 72, sec. 734(a) of the Foreign Relations Authorization Act, Fiscal Years 1994 and 1995 (P.L. 103-236; approved April 30, 1994), added paragraph about "presumption" in guidelines for presidential determination on transfers of MTCR Annex materials. In sec. 73, sec. 323(a) of the Foreign Relations Authorization Act, Fiscal Years 1992 and 1993 (P.L. 102-138; approved October 28, 1991), added assisting another country in acquiring missiles to the list of sanctionable acts; sec. 1136 of the Arms Control and Nonproliferation Act of 1999 (title XI of the Nance/Donovan Foreign Relations Authorization Act, Fiscal Years 2000 and 2001; H.R. 3427, enacted by reference in P.L. 106-113; approved November 29, 1999) added potential limitation on independent states of the former Soviet Union and the president's certification pertaining to judicial attention by MTCR adherents. Sec. 734(b) of the Foreign Relations Authorization Act, Fiscal Years 1994 and 1995 added the Director of the Arms Control and Disarmament Agency to those with whom the Secretary of State consults when administering the policy. This language, however, was struck out to conform with agency reorganization, particularly that of ACDA being incorporated into the State Department, by sec. 1136 of the Arms Control and Nonproliferation Act of 1999. Sec. 1408 of the National Defense Authorization Act for Fiscal Year 1996 (P.L. 104-106; approved February 10, 1996) made technical changes to reporting requirements relating to issuing a waiver.

Section 73B (Authority Relating to MTCR Adherents; 22 USC. 2797b-2) authorizes the president to impose sanctions against a foreign person, notwithstanding that person's operating in compliance with the laws of an MTCR adherent or that person exporting to an end-user in a country that is an MTCR adherent, if the country of jurisdiction over that foreign person is a country (1) that has entered into an understanding with the United States after January 1, 2000, (2) for which the United States retains the right to impose sanctions against those in the country's jurisdiction for exporting of controlled items that contribute to the acquisition, design, development, or production of missiles in a country that is not an MTCR adherent.

Sec. 1137 of the Arms Control and Nonproliferation Act of 1999 (title XI of the Nance/Donovan Foreign Relations Authorization Act, Fiscal Years 2000 and 2001; H.R. 3427, enacted by reference in P.L. 106-113; approved November 29, 1999) added sec. 73B, and made supporting amendments in sec. 73 relating to conditions of applicability, and sec. 74, defining "international understanding."

Section 74 (Definitions; 22 USC. 2797c) provides definitions of terms that also affect how the sanctions may be applied. For example, while the MTCR is a policy statement originally announced on April 16, 1987, by the United States, the United Kingdom, Germany, France, Italy, Canada, and Japan, the term "MTCR adherent" in this law is much more broadly defined, to include the countries that participate in the MTCR "or that, pursuant to an international understanding to which the United States is a party, controls MTCR equipment or technology in accordance with the criteria and standards set forth in the MTCR."[5] Within that definition, the term "international understanding" has been further defined to limit its applicability or to broaden the president's authority to impose sanctions. As another example, the term "person" has changed over time. The law formerly included as part of the definition of "person," "countries where it may be impossible to identify a specific governmental entity." This has been amended to refer to "countries with non-market economies (excluding former members of the Warsaw Pact)." The same definition formerly restricted government activity relating to development of aircraft; this now refers specifically to military aircraft.

Sec. 323 of the Foreign Relations Authorization Act, Fiscal Years 1992 and 1993 (P.L. 102-138; approved October 28, 1991), amended the definition of "person" to target China—the "Helms amendment"—and narrowed the definition of "person" to include activities of a government affecting the development of, among other things, "military aircraft" (formerly referred to "aircraft"). Sec. 1136(a) of the Arms Control and Nonproliferation Act of 1999 (title XI of the Nance/Donovan Foreign Relations Authorization Act, Fiscal Years 2000 and 2001; H.R. 3427, enacted by reference in P.L. 106-113; approved November 29, 1999) added the definition of "international understanding," a term used in the course of defining "MTCR adherent."

Section 81 ([CBW] Sanctions Against Foreign Persons; 22 USC. 2798) requires imposition of sanctions to deny government procurement, contracts with the U.S. government, and imports from foreign persons who knowingly and materially contribute, through exports from the United States or another country, or through other transactions, to foreign efforts to use, develop, produce, stockpile, or otherwise acquire chemical or biological weapons. Foreign persons are sanctionable if the recipient country has used chemical or biological weapons in violation of international law, has used chemical or biological weapons against its own people, or has made preparations to engage in such violations. Foreign persons are sanctionable if the recipient country has been determined to be a supporter of international terrorism, pursuant to section 6(j) of the Export Administration Act, or if the president has specifically designated the country as restricted under this section.

The president may delay the imposition of sanctions for up to 180 days if he is in consultation with the sanctionable person's government to bring that government to take specific and effective steps to terminate the sanctionable activities. The president may not be required to impose sanctions if the sanctionable person otherwise provides goods needed for U.S. military operations, if the president determines that the sanctionable person is a sole source provider of some good or service, or if the president determines that goods and services provided by the sanctionable person are essential to U.S. national security under defense cooperation agreements. Exceptions are also made for completing outstanding contracts, the purchase of spare or component parts, service and maintenance otherwise not readily available, information and technology essential to U.S. products or production, or medical or other humanitarian items.

The president may terminate the sanctions after 12 months if he determines and certifies to Congress that the sanctioned person no longer aids or abets any foreign government, project, or entity in its efforts to acquire biological or chemical weapons capability. The president may waive the application of a sanction after a year of its imposition if he determines it is in U.S. national security interests to do so. Not less than 20 days before a national security waiver is issued, the president must notify Congress, fully explaining the rationale for waiving the sanction.

Sec. 81 was added by sec. 305 of the Chemical and Biological Weapons Control and Warfare Elimination Act of 1991 (title III of P.L. 102-182; approved December 4, 1991.)[6]

Section 101 (Nuclear Enrichment Transfers; 22 USC. 2799aa) (similar to former section 669 of the Foreign Assistance Act of 1961) prohibits foreign economic or military assistance to any country that the president determines delivers or receives nuclear enrichment equipment, materials, or technology. The prohibition is not required if the countries involved in the transaction agree to place all materials, equipment, or technology under multilateral safeguard arrangements. The prohibition is not required, furthermore, if the recipient country has an agreement with the International Atomic Energy Agency (IAEA) regarding safeguards.

The president may waive the sanctions if he determines, and certifies to the Speaker of the House and the Senate Committee on Foreign Relations, that denying assistance would have a serious adverse effect on vital U.S. interests, and he has been assured that the country in question will not acquire, develop, or assist others in acquiring or developing nuclear weapons. Congress may negate a certification by enacting a joint resolution stating its disapproval.

Sec. 826(a) of the Nuclear Proliferation Prevention Act of 1994 (title VIII of the Foreign Relations Authorization Act, Fiscal Years 1994 and 1995; P.L. 103-236; approved April 30, 1994) added secs. 101 and 102. Similar language, however, previously had been in the Foreign Assistance Act of 1961, as secs. 669 and 670. Sec. 669, popularly referred to as the Symington amendment, was added by sec. 305 of the International Security Assistance and Arms Export Control Act of 1976 (P.L. 94-329; approved June 30, 1976).

Nuclear, Biological, Chemical, and Missile Proliferation Sanctions 75

The section was amended and restated by sec. 12 of the International Security Assistance Act of 1977 (P.L. 95-92; approved August 4, 1977), which also added sec. 670 to the law. Sec. 669 was further amended by secs. 10(b)(4) and 12 of the International Security Assistance Act of 1978 (P.L. 95-384; approved September 26, 1978). Sec. 737(b) of the International Security and Development Cooperation Act of 1981 (P.L. 97-113; approved December 29, 1981) amended and restated both secs. 669 and 670. Sec. 1204 of the International Security and Development Cooperation Act of 1985 (P.L. 99- 83; approved August 8, 1985), made further changes to sec. 670 before both sections were repealed in 1994 and similar language was incorporated into the AECA.

Section 102 (Nuclear Reprocessing Transfers, Illegal Exports for Nuclear Explosive Devices, Transfers of Nuclear Explosive Devices, and Nuclear Detonations; 22 USC. 2799aa-1) (similar to former section 670 of the Foreign Assistance Act of 1961) prohibits foreign economic or military assistance to countries that the president determines deliver or receive nuclear reprocessing equipment, material, or technology to or from another country; or any non-nuclear-weapon state that illegally exports, through a person serving as that country's agent, from the United States items that would contribute to nuclear proliferation.

The president may waive the sanctions if he determines, and certifies to the Speaker of the House and the Senate Committee on Foreign Relations, that terminating assistance would adversely impact on the United States' nonproliferation objectives, or would jeopardize the common defense and security. Congress may negate a certification by enacting a joint resolution stating its disapproval.

The section further prohibits assistance (except humanitarian or food assistance), defense sales, export licenses for U.S. Munitions List items, other export licenses subject to foreign policy controls (except medicines or medical equipment), and various credits and loans (except Department of Agriculture credits and support to procure food and agriculture commodities) to any country that the president has determined (A) transfers a nuclear explosive device to a nonnuclear-weapon state; (B) is a non-nuclear-weapon state and either (i) receives a nuclear explosive device; or (ii) detonates an nuclear explosive device; (C) transfers to a non-nuclear-weapon state any design information or component that is determined by the president to be important to, and known by the transferring country to be intended by the recipient state for use in, the development or manufacture of any nuclear explosive devices; or (D) is a non-nuclear-weapon state and seeks and receives any design information or component that is determined by the president to be important to, and intended by the recipient state for use in, the development or manufacture of any nuclear explosive device.

In any of these latter four instances, sanctions are mandatory once the president has determined that an event has occurred. If the event has to do with transferring a nuclear explosive device to a non-nuclear-weapon state, or a non-nuclear-weapon state receiving or detonating a nuclear explosive device, the president may delay the imposition of sanctions for 30 days (of congressional continuous session) if he determines that the immediate imposition of sanctions "would be detrimental to the national security of the United States," and so certifies to the Speaker of the House and the Chairperson of the Senate Committee on Foreign Relations.

If the president makes such a determination, he may further waive the imposition of sanctions if the Congress, within those 30 days after the first determination, takes up a joint resolution under expedited procedure,[7] that states:

> That the Congress having received on -------------a certification by the president under section 102(b)(4) of the Arms Export Control Act with respect to,----------------- the Congress hereby authorizes the president to exercise the waiver authority contained in section 102(b)(5) of that Act.

With passage of a joint resolution authorizing him to exercise further waiver authority, the president may waive any sanction that would otherwise be required in instances involving the transferring of a nuclear explosive device to a non-nuclear-weapon state, or a non-nuclear-weapon state receiving or detonating a nuclear explosive device. To exercise this waiver, the president determines and certifies in writing to the Speaker of the House and the Senate Committee on Foreign Relations "that the imposition of such sanction would be seriously prejudicial to the achievement of United State nonproliferation objectives or otherwise jeopardize the common defense and security."

Alternatively, if Congress does not take up a relevant joint resolution within the 30 days, the sanctions enter into effect. Section 102 does not state the means for otherwise suspending or terminating the sanctions.[8]

For legislative history of the origin of and early changes to this section, see discussion following sec. 101, above. Section 102, and sec. 670 before it, is popularly referred to as the Glenn amendment. Sec. 2(a) of the Agriculture Export Relief Act of 1998 (P.L. 105-194; approved July 14, 1998) broadened the kinds of exchanges that are exempt from the application of sanctions to include medicine, medical equipment, and Department of Agriculture financing.[9]

Waiver of Section 102, AECA, Sanctions Against North Korea

Section 1405 of the Military Construction, Veterans Affairs, and Related Agencies Appropriations, 2008 (P.L. 110- 252; approved June 30, 2008) (22 USC. 2799aa-1 note), provides:

SEC. 1405. (a) WAIVER AUTHORITY.—

(1) IN GENERAL.—Except as provided in subsection (b), the president may waive in whole or in part, with respect to North Korea, the application of any sanction contained in subparagraph (A), (B), (D) or (G) under section 102(b)(2) of the Arms Export Control Act (22 USC. 2799aa-1(b)), for the purpose of providing assistance related to—

A. the implementation and verification of the compliance by North Korea with its commitment, undertaken in the Joint Statement of September 19, 2005, to abandon all nuclear weapons and existing nuclear programs as part of the verifiable denuclearization of the Korean Peninsula; and

B. the elimination of the capability of North Korea to develop, deploy, transfer, or maintain weapons of mass destruction and their delivery systems.

(2) LIMITATION.—The authority under paragraph (1) shall expire 5 years after the date of enactment of this

Act.

(b) EXCEPTIONS.—

(1) LIMITED EXCEPTION RELATED TO CERTAIN SANCTIONS AND PROHIBITIONS.—The authority under subsection (a) shall not apply with respect to a sanction or prohibition under subparagraph (B) or (G) of section 102(b)(2) of the Arms Export Control Act, unless the president determines and certifies to the appropriate congressional committees that—

A. all reasonable steps will be taken to assure that the articles or services exported or otherwise provided will not be used to improve the military capabilities of the armed forces of North Korea; and

B. such waiver is in the national security interests of the United States.

(2) LIMITED EXCEPTION RELATED TO CERTAIN ACTIVITIES.— Unless the president determines and certifies to

A. the appropriate congressional committees that using the authority

> under subsection (a) is vital to the national security interests of the United States, such authority shall not apply with respect to—
>
> B. an activity described in subparagraph (A) of section 102(b)(1) of the Arms Export Control Act that occurs after September 19, 2005, and before the date of the enactment of this Act;
>
> C. an activity described in subparagraph (C) of such section that occurs after September 19, 2005; or an activity described in subparagraph (D) of such section that occurs after the date of enactment of this Act.
>
> (3) EXCEPTION RELATED TO CERTAIN ACTIVITIES OCCURRING AFTER DATE OF ENACTMENT.—The authority under subsection (a) shall not apply with respect to an activity described in subparagraph (A) or (B) of section 102(b)(1) of the Arms Export Control Act that occurs after the date of the enactment of this Act.
>
> (4) LIMITED EXCEPTION RELATED TO LETHAL WEAPONS.— The authority under subsection (a) shall not apply with respect to any export of lethal defense articles that would be prevented by the application of section 102(b)(2) of the Arms Export Control Act.
>
> (c) NOTIFICATIONS AND REPORTS.—* * *

Atomic Energy Act of 1954[10]

The Atomic Energy Act of 1954 declares U.S. policy for the development, use, and control of atomic energy. The Act authorizes the Nuclear Regulatory Commission to oversee the export of special nuclear materials and nuclear technology in accordance with bilateral and international cooperation agreements negotiated by the Department of State.

The Act defines the nature and requirements of those cooperative agreements and the procedure by which Congress reviews them. The Act states export licensing criteria for nuclear materials and sensitive equipment and technology.

Section 129 (Conduct Resulting in Termination of Nuclear Exports; 42 USC. 2158) prohibits the transfer of nuclear materials, equipment, or sensitive technology from the United States to any non-nuclear-weapon state that the president finds to have detonated a nuclear explosive device, terminated or abrogated safeguards of the International Atomic Energy Agency (IAEA), materially violated an IAEA safeguards agreement, or engaged in manufacture or acquisition of nuclear explosive devices. The section similarly

Nuclear, Biological, Chemical, and Missile Proliferation Sanctions 79

prohibits transfers to any country, or group of countries, that the president finds to have violated a nuclear cooperation agreement with the United States, assisted, encouraged, or induced a non-nuclear-weapon state to engage in certain activities related to nuclear explosive devices, or agreed to transfer reprocessing equipment, materials, or technology to a non-nuclear-weapon state, except under certain conditions.

The president may waive the restriction if he determines that the prohibition would hinder U.S. nonproliferation objectives or jeopardize the common defense and security.

Sixty days before a determination is issued, the president is required to forward his reasons for waiving the sanctions to Congress, which may block the waiver by adopting a joint resolution.

The section, as amended August 8, 2005, also prohibits the export, transfer, or licensing for export or transfer, of nuclear materials, nuclear equipment, or sensitive nuclear technology that could be applied to the design or construction of a nuclear reactor or nuclear weapon, to any country the government of which is cited as a supporter of acts of international terrorism, pursuant to sec. 620A(a) of the Foreign Assistance Act of 1961, sec. 6(j) of the Export Administration Act of 1979, or sec. 40(d) of the Arms Export Control Act.

The president may waive the restriction if he determines that to do so will not result in any increased risk that the targeted country will acquire a nuclear weapon, nuclear reactor, or any materials or components of a nuclear weapon.

The president's authority to waive sanctions also requires his determination and certification that the government of the country in question has not aided or abetted in the international proliferation of nuclear explosive devices or the acquisition of unsafeguarded nuclear materials within the past year, "has provided adequate, verifiable assurances that it will cease its support for acts of international terrorism," that waiving imposition is in the vital U.S. national security interest, or is "essential to prevent or respond to a serious radiological hazard in the country...that may or does threaten public health and safety."

Sec. 307 of the Nuclear Non-Proliferation Act of 1978 (P.L. 95-242; approved March 10, 1978) added sec. 129. Sec. 632(a) of the Energy Policy Act of 2005 (P.L. 109-58; approved August 8, 2005) added authorities related to restricting exports to a country the government of which is found to be a supporter of acts of international terrorism. Originally, the statute stated Congress could block a president's waiving of restrictions for common defense and security reasons by adopting a concurrent resolution; this was amended to *"joint resolution"* by sec. 203 of the U.S.- India Nuclear Cooperation Approval and Nonproliferation Enhancement Act (P.L. 110-369, approved October 8, 2008).

Chemical and Biological Weapons Control and Warfare Elimination Act of 1991[11]

The Chemical and Biological Weapons Control and Warfare Elimination Act of 1991 mandates U.S. sanctions, and encourages international sanctions, against countries that use chemical or biological weapons in violation of international law.

Section 307 (Sanctions Against Use of Chemical or Biological Weapons; 22 USC. 5605) requires the president to terminate foreign assistance (except humanitarian, food, and agricultural assistance), arms sales and licenses, credits, guarantees, and certain exports to a government of a foreign country that he has determined has used or made substantial preparation to use chemical or biological weapons.

Within three months, the president must determine and certify to Congress that the government: is no longer using chemical or biological weapons in violation of international law; is no longer using such weapons against its own people; has provided credible assurances that such behavior will not resume; and is willing to cooperate with U.N. or other international observers to verify that biological and chemical weapons are not still in use. Without this three-month determination, sanctions are required affecting multilateral development bank loans, U.S. bank loans or credits, exports, imports, diplomatic relations, and aviation access to and from the United States.

The president may lift the sanctions after a year, with a determination and certification to Congress that the foreign government has met the conditions listed above, and that it is making restitution to those affected by its use of chemical or biological weapons.

The president may waive the imposition of these sanctions if he determines and certifies to Congress and the appropriate committees that such a waiver is essential to U.S. national security interests.

The Chemical and Biological Weapons Control and Warfare Elimination Act of 1991 was enacted as title III of P.L. 102-182 (a law dealing with trade issues otherwise unrelated to nonproliferation). Sec. 1308 of the Foreign Relations Authorization Act, Fiscal Year 2003 (P.L. 107-228; approved

September 30, 2002) struck out reporting requirements that had been stated in sec. 308, as similar reports are required in other statutes.[12]

Chemical Weapons Convention Implementation Act of 1998[13]

The Chemical Weapons Convention Implementation Act of 1998 implements the Chemical Weapons Convention, which was originally signed on January 13, 1993, and to which the United States became a party on April 29, 1997.[14] The Convention bans the development, production, stockpiling, and use of chemical weapons, requires the destruction of existing weapons and related materials, establishes an international verification regime, and requires export controls and punitive measures to be leveled for noncompliance.

Section 103 (Civil Liability of the United States; 22 USC. 6713) requires a wide range of sanctions to be imposed, for a period of not less than ten years, on an individual who is a member of, or affiliated with, the Organization for the Prohibition of Chemical Weapons "whose actions or omissions the United States has been held liable for a tort or taking..."; or a foreign company or an individual affiliated with that company, "which knowingly assisted, encouraged, or induced, in any way, a foreign person" affiliated with the Organization "to publish, divulge, disclose, or make known in any manner or to any extent not authorized by the Convention any United States confidential business information" including:

- no arms export transactions—sales of items on U.S. Munitions List, transactions under Arms Export Control Act; no licenses for goods or services covered by foreign policy controls under the Export Administration Act of 1979;
- U.S. opposition to support in international financial institutions;
- no U.S. Export-Import Bank transactions;
- prohibition on U.S. private banks engaging with sanctioned person;
- assets in United States to be frozen by presidential action; and
- no rights to land aircraft in the United States (other than in cases of emergency).

The Secretary of State is further required to deny a visa to any individual affiliated with the Organization who divulges any confidential U.S. business if that disclosure results in financial loss or damages.

The section requires the president to impose similar sanctions on any foreign government found by the president to have similarly divulged such information, with the sanctions imposed for not less than five years. Foreign countries are further subject to:

- no U.S. economic assistance (other than humanitarian assistance), military assistance, foreign military financing, grant military education and training, military credits, guarantees; and no export licensing for commercial satellites.

Sanctions may be suspended if the sanctioned entity fully and completely compensates the U.S. government to cover the liability. The president, alternatively, may waive the sanctions if he determines and notifies Congress that U.S. national security interests are served by such a waiver.

Comprehensive Iran Sanctions, Accountability, and Divestment Act of 2010[15]

This Act, often referred to by its acronym—CISADA—substantively amends the Iran Sanctions Act of 1996, discussed elsewhere in this report. Several freestanding sections of CISADA, however, further codify restrictions on economic trade and transactions with Iran, and provide the president enhanced authority, and in some instances, require the president to take further steps, to isolate the government of Iran.

Section 103 (Economic Sanctions Relating to Iran; 22 USC. 8512) prohibits most imports and exports from Iran, and freezes Iranian assets that are under U.S. jurisdiction. The restrictions are redundant to steps taken by the president under the authority of the International Emergency Economic Powers Act (IEEPA), but in effect further codify the broadest restrictions on transactions with Iran. The section imposes these restrictions "notwithstanding section 101of the Iran Freedom Support Act," which codifies sanctions imposed by the president as of January 1, 2006, under authority granted his office in the IEEPA. The section requires the president to justify the import of any Iran-origin good on U.S. national interest grounds, and requires the president to certify this to Congress in advance of entering into such trade. He may also waive the application of sanctions if he finds it in the national interest to do so and certifies to Congress (under sec. 401).

Section 104 (Mandatory Sanctions With Respect to Financial Institutions That Engage in Certain Transactions; 22 USC. 8513) requires the Secretary of the Treasury, with consultation from the Secretary of State, to issue regulations "to prohibit, or impose strict conditions on, the opening or maintaining in the United States of a correspondent account or a payable-through account by a foreign financial institution that the Secretary finds knowingly" facilitates the efforts of Iran to acquire WMD or related delivery systems, supports any foreign terrorist organization, or supports acts of international terrorism; or facilitates the activities of a person subject to U.N. financial sanctions. The Secretary may waive the imposition of sanctions if he determines it in the national interest to do so and notifies Congress.

Section 302 (Identification of Countries of Concern With Respect to the Diversion of Certain Goods, Services, and Technologies to or through Iran; 22 USC. 8542) requires the Director of National Intelligence to identify countries of concern that are diverting to or through Iran goods, services, and technologies that are controlled or make a material contribution to Iran's WMD pursuits. Section 303 (Destinations of Diversion Concern; 22 USC. 8543) requires the president to designate any country of concern as a Destination of Diversion Concern if he determines that its government "allows substantial diversion of goods, services, or technologies ... to Iranian end-users or Iranian intermediaries." The president is required to report to Congress such determinations, and "shall require a license under the Export Administration Regulations or the International Traffic in Arms Regulations (whichever is applicable) to export to that country a good, service, or technology on the list required under subsection (b)(2), with the presumption that any application for such a license will be denied." The president may, however, delay the imposition of imposing licensing requirements if he finds the offending country is improving its own export control regime, indicting materials destined for Iran, complying with related U.N. Security Council resolutions, or meeting other standards. He may also waive the application of license controls if he finds it in the national interest to do so (under sec. 401). Section 304 (Report on Expanding Diversion Concern System to Address the Diversion of United States Origin Goods, Services, and Technologies to Certain Countries Other Than Iran) requires the president to report on broader diversion of U.S. Munitions List (USML) and Commerce Control List (CCL) items, and could ultimately serve as grounds for a new facet in the U.S. export control system.

Section 401 (General Provisions; 22 USC. 8551) terminates many of these authorities and the CISADA amendments to the Iran Sanctions Act of 1996 on the president's certification to Congress that Iran no longer supports acts of international terrorism and has "ceased the pursuit, acquisition, and development of nuclear, biological, and chemical weapons and ballistic missiles and ballistic missile launch technology."

P.L. 111-195; approved July 1, 2010. No amendments have been enacted.

Department of State, Foreign Operations, and Related Programs Appropriations Act, 2010[16]

An appropriations act funding Department of State and foreign operations programs is enacted annually—with rare exceptions when the previous year's legislation is continued through the next fiscal year by a continuing resolution—generally at the start of a fiscal year, to make appropriations for various foreign assistance, military assistance, and international financial institutions programs. Language enacted to fund programs in a current fiscal year act pertains only to that fiscal year unless otherwise expressly stated.

Congress has not enacted a comprehensive foreign aid authorization bill since 1985; however, as a result, the annual appropriations act increasingly has become a means of enacting authorizing language that carries the force of law beyond the fiscal year. In recent years, Security Assistance Acts and authorization acts addressing single issues have been enacted. Recent single-issue legislation has established the Millennium Challenge Corporation; authorized funding for microenterprise, HIV/AIDS, tuberculosis and malaria treatment and prevention programs, clean water, and programs for orphans and vulnerable children; transferred excess military equipment; established trafficking in persons as a human rights issue; and country-specific programs as a part of U.S. relations with North Korea, Afghanistan, Russia, and Sudan.

Title VI, Export and Investment Assistance, Export-Import Bank of the United States, prohibits the use of Export-Import Bank funds in the current fiscal year to make expenditures, contracts, or commitments for the export of nuclear equipment, fuel or technology to any nonnuclear-weapon state, if that state is otherwise eligible to receive economic or military assistance under this Act, but has detonated a nuclear explosive device after the date of enactment of this Act.

Title VII, General Provisions, Section 7043, Iran Sanctions, states that it is U.S. policy "to seek to prevent Iran from achieving the capability to produce or otherwise manufacture nuclear weapons...." The section prohibits the use of Export-Import Bank funds to guarantee, insure, or extend credit to any "energy producer or refiner that continues to ... provide Iran with significant refined

Nuclear, Biological, Chemical, and Missile Proliferation Sanctions   85

petroleum resources; ... materially contribute to Iran's capability to import refined petroleum resources; or ... allow Iran to maintain or expand ... its domestic production of refined petroleum resources...." This prohibition may be waived by the Secretary of State if she determines that the country targeted for these sanctions is "closely cooperating" with U.S. policy toward Iran. The president also retains the authority to waive the aid prohibition if he finds it important to U.S. national security interests to do so.

Title VII, General Provisions, Section 7073, Independent States of the Former Soviet Union, withholds 60 percent of funds allocated for Russia of the funds appropriated for "Assistance for Europe, Eurasia and Central Asia"—the Act provides $741,632,000 for the region (123 Stat. 3330)—until the president determines and certifies to the Committees on Appropriations that the Government of Russia has terminated its efforts "to provide Iran with technical expertise, training, technology, or equipment necessary to develop a nuclear reactor, related nuclear research facilities or programs, or ballistic missile capability ... and ... is providing full access to international non-government organizations providing humanitarian relief to refugees and internally displaced persons in Chechnya." The restriction does not apply to assistance for combating infectious diseases, child survival activities, assistance for victims of trafficking in persons, and nonproliferation and disarmament programs authorized under title V of the FREEDOM Support Act.

Congress has incorporated the language related to Export-Import Bank programs into the foreign assistance appropriations bill for several years. Iran-related text is new in FY2010. Russia-related text has been enacted in the foreign assistance appropriations measure since FY1999, though year-to-year the language has changed to make a comparison not particularly meaningful. In earlier years, the president was authorized to waive the restriction on the basis of vital U.S. national security interests, or if he found that the Government of Russia was taking meaningful steps to limit major supply contracts and to curtail the transfer of technology and technical expertise to certain programs in Iran. Beginning with the FY2006 Act, the latter condition was omitted.

Export Administration Act of 1979[17]

The Export Administration Act of 1979 (EAA) authorizes the executive branch to regulate private sector exports of particular goods and technology to other countries. The EAA coordinates such actions with other foreign policy considerations, including nonproliferation, and determines eligibility of recipients for exports. *Section 5 (National Security Controls; 50 USC. app. 2404)* authorizes the president to curtail or prohibit the export of any goods or services for national security reasons: to comply with other laws regarding a potential recipient country's political status or political stability; to cooperate with international agreements or understandings; or to protect militarily critical technologies. *Section 6 (Foreign Policy Controls; 50 USC. app. 2405)* similarly authorizes the president to curtail or prohibit the export of goods or services for foreign policy reasons. Within section 6, for example, *section 6(j)* establishes the State Department's list of countries found to be supporting acts of international terrorism, a list on which many other restrictions and prohibitions in law are based.[18] *Section 6(k)* restricts exportation of certain crime control equipment. *Section 6(l)* restricts exportation for a list of dual use goods and technology. *Section 6(m)* restricts exportation for a list of goods and technology that would directly and substantially assist a foreign government or group in acquiring the capability to develop, produce, stockpile, or deliver chemical or biological weapons.

Section 11A (Multilateral Export Control Violations; 50 USC. app. 2410a) requires the president to prohibit, for two to five years, the U.S. government from contracting with, or procuring goods or services from, a foreign person who has violated any country's national security export regulations in accordance with the agreement of the Coordinating Committee for Multilateral Export Controls (COCOM),[19] and that the violation results "in substantial enhancement of Soviet and East Bloc capabilities in submarines or antisubmarine warfare, ballistic or antiballistic missiles technology, strategic aircraft, command, control, communications and intelligence, or other critical technologies."

The president also is required generally to prohibit importation of products from the sanctioned person. The president may impose sanctions at his discretion if the first but not the second condition exists. In this case, the restrictions may be in place no longer than five years.

Sanctions may not be required for some goods if contracts with the sanctionable person meet U.S. operational military requirements, if the president determines that the sanctionable person is a sole source provider of an essential defense article or service, or if the president determines that such articles or services are essential to U.S. national security under defense coproduction agreements.

Nuclear, Biological, Chemical, and Missile Proliferation Sanctions   87

The president also may not be required to apply sanctions if he determines that a company affiliated with the sanctionable person had no knowledge of the export control violation. After sanctions have been in place for two years, the president may modify terms of the restrictions under certain conditions, and if he notifies Congress.

Sec. 2444 of the Multilateral Export Control Enhancement Amendments Act (title II, subtitle D, part II of the Omnibus Trade and Competitiveness Act of 1988; P.L. 100-418; approved August 23, 1988) added sec. 11A. The section has not been amended.

Section 11B (Missile Proliferation Control Violations; 50 USC. app. 2410b) is similar to sections 72 and 73 of the AECA, but authorizes sanctions against U.S. persons and foreign persons who engage in commercial transactions that violate missile proliferation controls. The section requires sanctions against any U.S. citizen whom the president determines to be engaged in exporting, transferring, conspiring to export or transfer, or facilitating an export or transfer of, any equipment or technology identified by the Missile Technology Control Regime Annex. Sanctions vary with the type of equipment or technology exported; worst-case sanctions deny export licenses for goods on controlled pursuant to the Export Administration Act for not less than two years.

The president may waive the imposition of sanctions if he certifies to Congress that the product or service to be restricted is essential to U.S. national security, and that the provider is a sole source provider.

The section further requires sanctions against any foreign person whom the president determines to be engaged in exporting, transferring, conspiring to export or transfer, or facilitating an export or transfer of, any MTCR equipment or technology that contributes to the design, development, or production of missiles in a country that is not an MTCR adherent. Sanctions vary with the type of equipment or technology exported; worst-case sanctions deny licenses for transfer to the foreign person items otherwise controlled by the Export Administration Act for not less than two years. The president may also prohibit importation into the United States of products produced by the foreign person.

The law allows several exceptions, wherein some or all of the sanctions may not be imposed against foreign persons. These exceptions are nearly identical to those found in sections 72 and 73 of the AECA. The president may waive the imposition of sanctions for national security reasons, but must notify Congress beforehand.

The presidential authority to restrict importation is conditional in a manner identical to that in section 73 of the AECA. The definition of "MTCR adherent" in section 11B is also identical to that in section 74 of the AECA. The definition of "person," however, retains its earlier form, applying to all "countries where it may be impossible to identify a specific governmental entity," and not adopting the narrower reference to military aircraft but referring to government activity relating to development of aircraft generally.

Sec. 1702(b) of the National Defense Authorization Act for Fiscal Year 1991 (P.L. 101-510; approved November 5, 1990) added sec. 11B. The section has not been amended.

Section 11C (Chemical and Biological Weapons Proliferation Sanctions; 50 USC. app. 2410c), similar to section 81 of the AECA, authorizes the president to apply procurement and import sanctions against foreign persons that he determines knowingly contribute to the use, development, production, stockpile, or acquisition of chemical or biological weapons by exporting goods or technology from the United States or any other country.

The president may delay the imposition of sanctions for up to 180 days if he is in consultation with the sanctionable person's government to bring that government to take specific and effective steps to terminate the sanctionable activities.

The president may not be required to impose or maintain sanctions if the sanctionable person otherwise provides goods needed for U.S. military operations, if the president determines that the sanctionable person is a sole source provider of some good or service, or if the president determines that goods and services provided by the sanctionable person are essential to U.S. national security under defense cooperation agreements. Exceptions are also made for completing outstanding contracts, the purchase of spare or component parts, service and maintenance otherwise not readily available, information and technology essential to U.S. products or production, or medical or other humanitarian items.

The president may terminate the sanctions after 12 months, if he determines and certifies to Congress that the sanctioned person no longer aids or abets any foreign government, project, or entity in its efforts to acquire biological or chemical weapons capability.

The president may waive the application of a sanction after a year of its imposition, if he determines it is in U.S. national security interests to do so. Not less than 20 days before a national security waiver is issued, the president must notify Congress, fully explaining the rationale for waiving the sanction.

Nuclear, Biological, Chemical, and Missile Proliferation Sanctions 89

Sec. 505(a) of the Chemical and Biological Weapons Control and Warfare Elimination Act of 1991 (title III of P.L. 102-182; approved December 4, 1991) added sec. 11C. No amendments have been enacted.

Export-Import Bank Act of 1945[20]

The Export-Import Bank Act of 1945 establishes the Export-Import Bank of the United States and authorizes the Bank to finance and facilitate exports and imports and the exchange of commodities and services between the United States and foreign countries.

Section 2(b)(1)(B) (12 USC. 635(b)(1)(B)) generally states the United States' policy of administering loan programs through the Export-Import Bank. The section provides that the Bank will deny applications for credit for nonfinancial or noncommercial considerations only when the president determines it is in the U.S. national interest to deny credit to advance U.S. policies in international terrorism—including taking into account a nation's lack of cooperation in efforts to eradicate terrorism—nuclear proliferation, environmental protection, and human rights.

Sec. 2(b)(1) was amended and restated in 1972 (P.L. 92-126) and again in 1974 (P.L. 93-646). The language pertaining to international terrorism and nuclear proliferation was added by sec. 1904 of the Export-Import Bank Act Amendments of 1978 (title XIX of the Financial Institutions Regulatory and Interest Rate Control Act of 1978; P.L. 95-630; approved November 10, 1978). The Export-Import Bank Reauthorization Act of 2002 (P.L. 107-189; approved June 14, 2002) added a reference to the Universal Declaration of Human Rights adopted by the United Nations General Assembly on December 10, 1948 (sec. 15), added language pertaining to a nation's lack of cooperation with efforts to eradicate terrorism (sec. 17), and added enforcement of the Foreign Corrupt Practices Act, the Arms Export Control Act, the International Emergency Economic Powers Act, or the Export Administration Act of 1979, as justification for denying Export-Import Bank financing (sec. 21). Numerous technical changes were made by P.L. 107-189, as well.

Section 2(b)(4) (12 USC. 635(b)(4)) provides that the Secretary of State can determine, and report to Congress[21] and to the Export-Import Bank Directors, if:

- any country has agreed to IAEA nuclear safeguards but has materially violated, abrogated, or terminated such safeguards after October 26, 1977;
- any country has entered into a cooperation agreement with the United States concerning the use of civil nuclear energy, but has violated, abrogated, or terminated any guarantee or other undertaking related to that agreement after October 26, 1977;
- any country has detonated a nuclear explosive device after October 26, 1977, but is a not a nuclear-weapon state;
- any country willfully aids or abets, after June 29, 1994, any non-nuclear-weapon state to acquire a nuclear explosive device or to acquire unsafeguarded special nuclear material; or
- any person knowingly aids or abets, after September 23, 1996, any non-nuclear-weapon state to acquire a nuclear explosive device or to acquire unsafeguarded special nuclear material.

If such a determination is made relating to a person, the Secretary is urged to consult with that person's government to curtail that person's activities. Consultations are allowed 90 days, at the end of which the Secretary will report to Congress as to their progress. After the 90 days, unless the Secretary requests an additional 90 days, or unless the Secretary reports that the violations have ceased, the Export-Import Bank will not approve any transactions to support U.S. exports to any country, or to or by any person, for which/whom a determination has been made. The imposition of sanctions may also be waived if the president, 45 days before any transaction is approved, certifies that the violations have ceased, and that steps have been taken to ensure the questionable transactions will not resume. The president may also waive the imposition of sanction if he certifies that to impose them would have a serious adverse effect on vital U.S. interests, or if he certifies that the objectionable behavior has ceased.

Sec. 2(b)(4) was added by sec. 3(b) of P.L. 95-143; approved October 26, 1977. Sec. 825 of the Nuclear Proliferation Prevention Act of 1994 (title VIII of the Foreign Relations Authorization Act, Fiscal Years 1994 and 1995; P.L. 103-236; approved April 30, 1994) added "(as defined in section 830(4) of the Nuclear Proliferation Prevention Act of 1994), or that any country has willfully aided or abetted any non-nuclear-weapons state (as defined in section 830(5) of that Act) to acquire any such nuclear explosive device or to acquire unsafeguarded special nuclear material (as defined in section 830(8) of that Act)" to define "nuclear explosive device" and to broaden what acts are

Nuclear, Biological, Chemical, and Missile Proliferation Sanctions 91

sanctionable. This is often referred to as a "Glenn Amendment" (but not to be confused with "the Glenn Amendment," which, by all accounts, would be sec. 102 of the AECA). The section was further amended and restated by sec. 1303 of the National Defense Authorization Act for Fiscal Year 1997 (P.L. 104-201; approved September 23, 1996). Sec. 1303(b) of that Act further required the president to report to Congress within 180 days "his recommendations on ways to make the laws of the United States more effective in controlling and preventing the proliferation of weapons of mass destruction and missiles. The report shall identify all sources of government funds used for such nonproliferation activities."

Section 2(b)(12) (12 USC. 635(b)(12)) requires the president to notify the Export-Import Bank if he determines "that the military or Government of the Russian Federation has transferred or delivered to the People's Republic of China an SS-N-22 missile system and that the transfer or delivery represents a significant and imminent threat to the security of the United States... Upon receipt of the notice and if so directed by the president of the United States, the Board of Directors of the Bank shall not give approval to guarantee, insure, extend credit, or participate in the extension of credit in connection with the purchase of any good or service by the military or Government of the Russian Federation."

Sec. 12 of the Export-Import Bank Reauthorization Act of 1997 (P.L. 105-121; approved November 26, 1997) added paragraph 12.

Foreign Assistance Act of 1961[22]

The Foreign Assistance Act of 1961 (FAA) authorizes U.S. government foreign aid programs including development assistance, economic support funding, numerous multilateral programs, housing and other credit guaranty programs, Overseas Private Investment Corporation, international organizations, debt-for-nature exchanges, international narcotics control, international disaster assistance, development funding for Africa, assistance to states of the former Soviet Union, military assistance, international military education and training, peacekeeping, antiterrorism, and various regional enterprise funds.

Section 307(c) (Withholding of United States Proportionate Share for Certain Programs of International Organizations; 22 USC. 2227) requires that foreign assistance the United States pays in to international organizations and programs not be used for programs in certain countries. The section exempts the International Atomic Energy Agency (IAEA) from this limitation,[23] except for particular projects the IAEA finances in Cuba. U.S. proportionate support to the IAEA, in particular, is not available to any IAEA project relating to the Juragua Nuclear Power Plant near Cienfugeos, Cuba, or the Pedro Pi Nuclear Research Center in Cuba, unless Cuba: ratifies the Treaty on Non-Proliferation of Nuclear Weapons or the Treaty of Tlatelelco and is in compliance with terms of the treaty; negotiates full-scope safeguards of the IAEA not later than two years after treaty ratification; and "incorporates internationally accepted nuclear safety safeguards."

Section 307 was added to the Foreign Assistance Act of 1961 by sec. 403 of the International Security and Development Cooperation Act of 1985 (P.L. 99-83; approved August 8, 1985). The countries to which it is applied has changed over time; the countries for which program funding is currently restricted are Burma, North Korea, Syria, Iran, Cuba, and the Palestine Liberation Organization (though application to the PLO has been waived under other legislation in the course of peace negotiations), and communist countries listed under sec. 620(f) of the Act (currently North Korea, China, Cuba, Vietnam, and Tibet). Most recently, sec. 616 of the Department of State, Foreign Operations, and Related Programs Appropriations Act, 2008 (division J of P.L. 110-161; 121 Stat. 2320) removed Libya from the sec. 307 list.[24] Limitations in subsec. (c) were originally added by sec. 431(a)(2) of the Foreign Relations Authorization Act, 1994 and 1995 (P.L. 103-236; approved April 30, 1994). Language pertaining to nuclear developments in Cuba was added by sec. 2809(a)(1) of the Foreign Relations Authorization Act, 1998 and 1999 (subdivision B of division G of P.L. 105-277; approved October 21, 1998).

Section 498A(b) (Criteria for Assistance to Governments of the Independent States [of the Former Soviet Union]; 22 USC. 2295a(b)) requires that the president not provide assistance to independent states of the former Soviet Union if he determines that the government of that state, among other things, (1) has failed to implement arms control obligations signed by the former Soviet Union, or (2) has knowingly transferred to another country: missiles or missile technology inconsistent with guidelines and parameters of the Missile Technology Control Regime; "any material, equipment, or technology that would contribute significantly to the ability of such country to manufacture any weapon of mass destruction (including nuclear, chemical, and biological weapons) if the president determines that the material, equipment, or technology was to be used by such country in the manufacture of such weapon." The section further prohibits foreign assistance under chapter 11 of the Foreign Assistance Act of 1961 to any country for which a determination has been issued pursuant to sections 101 or 102 of the Arms Export Control Act or sections 306(a)(1) or 307 of the Chemical and Biological Weapons Control and Warfare Elimination Act of 1991.

The president may waive the prohibition—other than that based on other proliferation legislation as cited in the section—on U.S. national security grounds, if he determines that furnishing assistance "will foster respect for internationally recognized human rights and the rule of law or the development of institutions of democratic governance," or to alleviate suffering resulting from a natural or man-made disaster. Assistance may also be provided under the U.S. Information Agency's (USIA) secondary school exchange program notwithstanding a country's ineligibility (except in instances where ineligibility is based on nonproliferation violations). Any waiver requires an immediate report to Congress of any determination or decision.

Section 498A was added by sec. 201 of the FREEDOM Support Act (P.L. 102-511; approved October 24, 1992). See also discussion, above, on sec. 73(b)(2) and sec. 73B of the AECA, as amended. Those sections refer to sec. 498A(b)(3)(A) to limit certain transactions with independent states of the former Soviet Union if the transactions involve missiles or missile technology and are conducted in a manner inconsistent with guidelines and parameters of the MTCR. Sec. 106 of the Liberty and Democratic Solidarity (LIBERTAD) Act of 1996 (P.L. 104- 114; adopted March 12, 1996) added requirements to curtail assistance to any third country engaged in certain support of Cuba.

Section 620(y) (Prohibitions Against Furnishing Assistance; 22 USC. 2370) restricts foreign assistance, or assistance pursuant to any other act, to any country providing nuclear fuel, related assistance, and credits to Cuba. Assistance denied the country in question equals the value of that country's nuclear development assistance, sales, or transfers to Cuba. The requirement to limit assistance is waived if Cuba (A) ratifies the Treaty on Non-Proliferation of Nuclear Weapons or the Treaty of Tlatelelco and is in compliance with terms of the treaty; (B) "has negotiated and is in full compliance with full-scope safeguards of the International Atomic Energy Agency" within two years of the treaty ratification; and (C) "incorporates and is in compliance with internationally accepted nuclear safety safeguards." The section also requires the Secretary of State to report to Congress annually on the matter.

Added by sec. 2810(a) of the Foreign Relations Authorization Act, Fiscal Years 1998 and 1999 (subdivision B of Division G of P.L. 105-277; approved October 21, 1998).

Section 620E (Assistance to Pakistan; 22 USC. 2375), related to U.S. assistance to Pakistan, was enacted in response to the threat posed by Soviet occupation of neighboring Afghanistan. *Section 620E(d)* authorizes the president to waive sanctions under section 101 of the AECA to provide assistance to Pakistan, if he determines it is in the U.S. national interest to do so.

Subsection 620E(e) states that no military assistance shall be furnished and no military equipment or technology shall be sold or transferred to Pakistan unless the president certifies to the Speaker of the House and the Chairperson of the Senate Foreign Relations Committee that, for the fiscal year in which the assistance, sale or transfer would occur, Pakistan does not possess a nuclear explosive device and that proposed military assistance would significantly reduce the risk that Pakistan will possess a nuclear explosive device. This restriction does not apply to international narcotics control assistance, International Military Education and Training funds, funding for humanitarian and civic assistance projects, peacekeeping or other multilateral operations funds, or antiterrorism assistance.

Sec. 620E was added to the Foreign Assistance Act of 1961 by sec. 736 of the International Security and Development Cooperation Act of 1981 (P.L. 97-113; approved December 29, 1981). Sec. 620E(d) was amended by the Nuclear Proliferation Prevention Act of 1994 (title VIII of the Foreign Relations Authorization Act, Fiscal Years 1994 and 1995; P.L. 103-236; approved April 30, 1994) to reflect the repeal of secs. 669 and 670 and the enactment of secs. 101 and 102 of the Arms Export Control Act. Sec. 620E(e), the "Pressler amendment," was added by sec. 902 of the International Security and Development Cooperation Act of 1985 (P.L. 99-83; approved August 8, 1985). Sec. 559(a)(1)(D) of the Foreign Operations, Export Financing, and Related Programs Appropriations Act, 1996 (P.L. 104-107; approved February 12, 1996), amended the section to exclude certain assistance programs from the ban, as noted in the last sentence, above. The same Act amended the section to authorize the president to: release Pakistan from paying storage costs of items purchased before October 1, 1990, but not delivered (presumably F-16s); release other items serviced in the United States; and continue the applicability of other laws pertaining to ballistic missile sanctions. This bloc of amendments is sometimes referred to as the "Brownback amendment." The same Act made several changes to restrict only "military assistance," formerly the section had referred to assistance generally; this amendment is popularly referred to as the "Brown amendment."

After India and Pakistan tested nuclear explosive devices in May 1998, sanctions were imposed in accordance with requirements of sec. 102 of the Arms Export Control Act (see above). Subsequently, Congress enacted several laws to ease sanctions or to grant the president discretionary authority to waive their application. The Agriculture Export Relief Act of 1998 (P.L. 105-194; approved July 14, 1998) authorizes the exemption of sanctions as they pertain to certain agricultural commodities. The India-Pakistan Relief Act (title IX of the Agriculture, Rural Development, Food and Drug Administration, and Related Agencies Appropriations Act, 1999; division A, sec. 101(a) of P.L. 105-277; 112 Stat. 2681-40; approved October 21, 1998) authorizes the president to waive the application of most sanctions under secs. 101 and 102 of the AECA, sec. 620E(e) of the Foreign Assistance Act of 1961, and sec. 2(b)(4) of the Export-Import Bank Act of 1945, for a period of one year. The Department of Defense Appropriations Act, 2000 (P.L. 106-79; approved October 21, 1999; see title IX), repeals the India-Pakistan Relief Act, but also authorizes the president to waive the same sections of law, including sec. 620E(e). President Clinton exercised this authority in issuing Presidential Determination No. 2000-4 on October 27, 1999 (64 F.R. 60649) to the extent it applied, in the case of Pakistan, to "credit, credit guarantee, or other financial assistance provided by the Department of Agriculture to support the purchase of food or other agricultural commodity; and the making of any loan or the providing of any credit to the Government of Pakistan by any U.S. bank." On September 22, 2001, President Bush lifted all remaining nuclear test-related sanctions against India and Pakistan, including sec. 620E(e), under the authority granted him in P.L. 106-79 (Presidential Determination No. 2001- 28; 66 F.R. 50095).

Other measures addressed sanctions imposed on Pakistan for other reasons. P.L. 107-57 (115 Stat. 403, approved October 27, 2001), authorizes the president to waive remaining restrictions (relating to military dictatorship and debt arrearage, statutorily required by the Foreign Assistance Act of 1961 and annual foreign operations appropriations measures) on foreign assistance to Pakistan. P.L. 108-447 (of which division D is the Foreign Operations, Export Financing, and Related Programs Appropriations Act, 2005; approved December 8, 2004), amends P.L. 107-57 to extend foreign assistance to Pakistan to October 1, 2005. P.L. 108-458 (of which title VII is the 9/11 Commission Implementation Act of 2004; approved December 17, 2004), sought to amend P.L. 107-57 to extend foreign aid to Pakistan to October 1, 2006. This amendment, however, was not executable for technical reasons. Sec. 117 of the Continuing Resolution (P.L. 109-77; 119 Stat. 2037; approved

September 30, 2005), and subsequently, sec. 534 of the Foreign Operations, Export Financing, and Related Programs Appropriations Act, 2006 (P.L. 109-102; 119 Stat 2210, approved November 14, 2005), however, authorizes the president to waive the applicability to Pakistan of restrictions imposed on a country under military dictatorship and waives debt arrearage requirements for Fiscal Year 2006. Authorities contained in P.L. 109-102, in turn, were continued into fiscal year 2007 by division B of P.L. 109- 289 (120 Stat. 1257 at 1311; approved September 29, 2006), as amended.

Henry J. Hyde United States-India Peaceful Atomic Energy Cooperation Act of 2006[25]

The Hyde U.S.-India Peaceful Atomic Energy Cooperation Act of 2006 exempts some requirements of the Atomic Energy Act of 1954 in order for the president to negotiate a U.S.- India nuclear cooperation agreement. The Act reaffirms the United States' commitment to the Nuclear Non-Proliferation Treaty (to which India is not a signatory) and adherence to Nuclear Suppliers Group guidelines. The Act authorizes the Secretary of Energy, with consultation from the Secretaries of State and Defense, to "establish a cooperative nuclear nonproliferation program to pursue jointly with scientists from the United States and India a program to further common nuclear nonproliferation goals." The Act also implements a new U.S. Additional Protocol to the Nuclear Non-Proliferation Treaty, signed on June 12, 1998, to demonstrate the United States' commitment to the Treaty and to encourage non-nuclear-weapon states to commit to international nuclear nonproliferation standards.

Section 104(d)(3) (Waiver Authority and Congressional Approval; Restrictions on Nuclear Transfers; Termination of Nuclear Transfers to India; 22 USC. 8003(d)(3)) terminates exports of nuclear and nuclear-related material, equipment, or technology to India if, after the proposed U.S.-India nuclear cooperation agreement enters into force, any Indian person transfers: "(i) nuclear or nuclear-related material, equipment, or technology that is not consistent with NSG guidelines or decisions, or (ii) ballistic missiles or missile-related equipment or technology that is not consistent with MTCR guidelines."

The president may determine "that cessation of such exports would be seriously prejudicial to the achievement of United States nonproliferation objectives or otherwise jeopardize the common defense and security" to allow nuclear-related exports to India to continue. The president may also allow exports to continue if he finds that (i) the transfer in question was made without the knowledge of the Government of India; (ii) at the time of the transfer, either the Government of India did not own, control, or direct the Indian person that made the transfer or the Indian person that made the transfer is a natural person who acted without the knowledge of a Indian commercial or government entity ; and "(iii) the president certifies to the appropriate congressional committees that the Government of India has taken or is taking appropriate judicial or other enforcement actions against the Indian person with respect to such transfer."

Sec. 106. (Inoperability of Determination and Waivers; 22 USC. 8005) cancels any waiver or determination issued under section 104 "if the president determines that India has detonated a nuclear explosive device after the date of the enactment of this title."

Secs. 101 and 105 of the United States-India Nuclear Cooperation Approval and Nonproliferation Enhancement Act (P.L. 110-369; approved October 8, 2008) modified sunset and report provisions in the Hyde Act.

International Emergency Economic Powers Act[26]

Section 203 (Grants of Authorities; 50 USC. 1702) authorizes the president "to deal with any unusual and extraordinary threat with respect to a declared national emergency."[27] After he declares a national emergency exists, pursuant to the authority in the National Emergencies Act, the president may use the authority in this section to investigate, regulate, or prohibit foreign exchange transactions, credit transfers or payments, currency or security transfers, and may take specified actions relating to property in which a foreign country or person has interest. In terms of nonproliferation concerns, it is pursuant to this section that the president has continued the authority of the expired Export Administration Act, prohibited transactions with "those who disrupt the Middle East peace process," issued export controls on encryption items, established export controls related to weapons of mass destruction, prohibited transactions "with persons who commit, threaten to commit, or support terrorism," and blocked certain property of, and transactions with, governments of specific countries found to be engaged in activities that constitute an extraordinary threat,[28] including the proliferation of weapons of mass destruction (see Table 1 for the proliferation-based exercise of IEEPA authorities and Table 2 for an index of regulations implementing those authorities).

Enacted as title II of P.L. 95-223; approved December 28, 1977, to update and continue authority carried earlier in the Trading With the Enemy Act (P.L. 65-92; approved October 6, 1917). It has been amended from time to time to update the list of what cannot be restricted, mostly to keep up with changes in technology (for example, the law allows the free flow of informational materials, most recently amended to include CD ROMs). Most recently, the USA PATRIOT Act (P.L. 107-56; approved October 26, 2001) made amendments to clarify the applicability of the IEEPA to persons or property subject to the jurisdiction of the United States, and to make available any classified materials in court proceedings related to IEEPA violations.

Table 1. Executive Orders Issued Pursuant to IEEPA Authorities in Furtherance of Nonproliferation Objectives

Executive Order	Purpose
12938, as amended (November 14, 1994; 59 F.R. 59099)	Proliferation of weapons of mass destruction
12947, as amended (January 23, 1995; 60 F.R. 5079)	Prohibiting transactions with terrorists who threaten to disrupt the Middle East peace process (relating to those who commit "grave acts of violence")
12957, as amended (March 15, 1995; 60 F.R. 14615)	Prohibiting certain transactions with respect to the development of Iranian petroleum resources
12959, as amended (May 6, 1995; 60 F.R. 24757)	Prohibiting certain transactions with respect to the development of Iranian petroleum resources
13059, as amended (August 19, 1997; 62 F.R. 44531)	Prohibiting certain transactions with respect to Iran
13159 (June 21, 2000; 65 F.R. 39279)	Blocking property of the Government of the Russian Federation relating to the disposition of highly enriched uranium extracted from nuclear weapons
13222(August 17, 2001; 66 F.R. 44025)	Continuation of export control regulations (with the expiration of the Export Administration Act of 1979)
13338, as amended(May 11, 2004; 69 F.R. 26751)	Blocking property of certain persons and prohibiting export of certain goods to Syria (relating to pursuit of weapons of mass destruction, terrorism, occupation of Lebanon, and stability in Iraq)
13382(June 28, 2005; 70 F.R. 38567)	Blocking property of weapons of mass destruction proliferators and their supporters

Nuclear, Biological, Chemical, and Missile Proliferation Sanctions   99

Executive Order	Purpose
13466(June 26, 2008; 73 F.R. 36787)	Continuing certain restrictions with respect to North Korea and North Korean Nationals (imposed on the same day the designation as a state sponsor of acts of international terrorism and Trading With the Enemy Act restrictions were lifted)
13551(August 30, 2010; 75 F.R. 53837)	Blocking Property of Certain Persons With Respect to North Korea
13553(September 28, 2010; 75 F.R. 60587)	Blocking Property of Certain Persons With Respect to Serious Human Rights Abuses by the Government of Iran and Taking Certain Other Actions (in part implements the requirements of the Comprehensive Iran Sanctions, Accountability, and Divestment Act of 2010)

Source: The National Archives prints executive orders in the Federal Register and maintains a database of orders and subsequent amendments at http://www. archives.gov/federal-register/executive-orders/disposition.html.

Notes: 50 USC. 1701 note. The president also uses the authority in IEEPA to issue executive orders to implement United Nations Security Council Resolutions, some of which are the result of proliferation concerns, currently including multilateral sanctions applied against Iran and North Korea.

Table 2. Selected Regulations Implementing IEEPA Authorities in Furtherance of Nonproliferation Objectives

Regulation	Department and Agency / Purpose
15 CFR Part 700	Department of Commerce, Bureau of Industry and Security • Chemical Weapons Convention regulations (parts 710-722) • Export Administration regulations (EAR; parts 730-780), including: Commerce Control List (CCL) overview and the Country Chart, 15 CFR 738.1 et seq.; CCL-based controls, 15 CFR 742.1 et seq.; embargoes and other special controls, 15 CFR 746.1 et seq.; and the CCL, 15 CFR 774.1 et seq.
31 CFR Part 500	Department of the Treasury, Office of Foreign Assets Control Foreign assets control regulations
31 CFR Part 501	Department of the Treasury, Office of Foreign Assets Control Reporting, procedures, penalties
31 CFR Part 510	Department of the Treasury, Office of Foreign Assets Control North Korea assets

Table 2. (Continued)

Regulation	Department and Agency / Purpose
31 CFR Part 535	Department of the Treasury, Office of Foreign Assets Control Iran assets
31 CFR Part 539	Department of the Treasury, Office of Foreign Assets Control Weapons of mass destruction trade
31 CFR Part 540	Department of the Treasury, Office of Foreign Assets Control Highly enriched uranium (HEU) agreement assets
31 CFR Part 542	Department of the Treasury, Office of Foreign Assets Control Syria sanctions
31 CFR Part 544	Department of the Treasury, Office of Foreign Assets Control Weapons of mass destruction proliferators sanctions
31 CFR Part 549	Department of the Treasury, Office of Foreign Assets Control Lebanon sanctions
31 CFR Part 560	Department of the Treasury, Office of Foreign Assets Control Iran transactions
31 CFR Part 561	Department of the Treasury, Office of Foreign Assets Control Iran transactions

Source: Code of Federal Regulations.
Notes: 50 USC. 1701 note.

Iran Freedom Support Act[29]

Section 101 (Codification of Sanctions) locks in place the substantive elements of three Executive orders in effect on January 1, 2006.[30] The orders, first issued by President Clinton in 1995 and 1997, and renewed annually by him and then by his successors, impose economic sanctions on transactions and trade with Iran, including prohibiting any U.S. person from: entering into a contract or financing related to the development of petroleum resources in Iran; making new investments in property owned or controlled by the Government of Iran; or exporting goods or technology to Iran, investing there, or engaging in transactions to traffic Iran-made goods or technology.

The executive orders were issued by the president under authority granted his office in the National Emergencies Act and the International Emergency Economic Powers Act. To terminate the sanctions, the president is now required to notify Congress 15 days in advance, unless circumstances require the president to first terminate sanctions and notify Congress after the fact, but

Nuclear, Biological, Chemical, and Missile Proliferation Sanctions 101

then within three days after exercising the authority. In effect, the section dampens the president's authority to lift the sanctions on Iran without advising Congress, though notification is the only requirement to satisfy the law.

Iran-Iraq Arms Nonproliferation Act of 1992[31]

Section 1603 (Application to Iran of Certain Iraq Sanctions) makes sanctions in section 586G(a)(1) through (4) of the Iraq Sanctions Act of 1990 also fully applicable against Iran (see below, including notes as they pertain to Iraq).

Section 1604 (Sanctions Against Certain Persons) requires the president to impose sanctions against any person whom he has determined to be engaged in transferring goods or technology so as to contribute knowingly and materially to the efforts by Iran or Iraq to acquire chemical, biological, nuclear, or destabilizing numbers and types of advanced conventional weapons. Section 1605 (Sanctions Against Certain Foreign Countries) similarly addresses activities of foreign governments.

In both cases, mandatory sanctions prohibit, for a period of two years, the U.S. government from entering into procurement agreements with, or issuing licenses for exporting to or for the sanctioned person or country. Where a foreign country is found to be in violation of the law, the president must suspend U.S. assistance; instruct U.S. Executive Directors in the international financial institutions to oppose multilateral development bank assistance; suspend codevelopment and coproduction projects the U.S. government might have with the offending country for one year; suspend, also for one year, most technical exchange agreements involving military and dual-use technology; and prohibit the exportation of U.S. Munitions List items for one year. In the case of foreign countries targeted for sanctions under this Act, the president may, at his discretion, use authority granted him under the International Emergency Economic Powers Act to further prohibit transactions with the country.

The president may waive the mandatory sanctions against persons or foreign country with 15 days notice to congressional committees that exercising such a waiver is essential to U.S. national interests.

Enacted as title XVI of the National Defense Authorization Act for Fiscal Year 1993 (P.L. 102- 484; approved October 23, 1992). Sec. 1408(a) of P.L. 104-106 (110 Stat. 494) amended sections 1604 and 1605 to apply not just to conventional weapons but also to chemical, biological, or nuclear weapons.

Sec. 1308 of the Foreign Relations Authorization Act, Fiscal Year 2003 (P.L. 107-228; approved September 30, 2002) consolidated various reports related to missile proliferation and essential components of nuclear, biological, chemical, and radiological weapons in one section of law, and repealed language in other sections of law, including a report required under sec. 1607 of this Act, to result in fewer reports overall.

Iran, North Korea, and Syria Nonproliferation Act of 2000[32]

Sections 2 through 5 (Reports; Application; Procedures; Determination; 50 USC. 1701 note) require the president to report to Congress twice a year to identify "every foreign person with respect to whom there is credible information indicating that the person, on or after January 1, 1999, transferred to or acquired from Iran, or on or after January 1, 2005, transferred to or acquired from Syria..." goods, services or technology the export of which (1) is controlled for nonproliferation reasons in accordance with various international agreements, or (2) is not controlled by the country of origin but would be subject to controls if shipped from the United States. The president is authorized to apply a range of sanctions against any foreign person included in his report, including denial of procurement contracts with the U.S. government, prohibition on importation into the United States, and denial of foreign assistance—sanctions laid out in Executive Order 12938, as amended.[33] A foreign person named in the president's report may also be denied U.S. government sales of items on the U.S. Munitions List and export licenses for dual-use items.

The decision to impose sanctions is left to the president, but if he decides to take no action, he is required to notify Congress of his reasons. The president may also take no action if he finds that (1) the person in question did not "knowingly transfer to or acquire from Iran or Syria" objectionable items; (2) the goods, services or technology "did not materially contribute to the efforts of Iran or Syria, as the case may be, to develop nuclear, biological, or chemical weapons, or ballistic or cruise missile systems, or weapons listed on the Wassenaar Arrangement Munitions List..."; (3) the named person falls under the jurisdiction of a government that is an adherent to "one or more relevant nonproliferation regimes" and his actions were consistent with such regime's guidelines; or (4) the government of jurisdiction "has imposed meaningful penalties" on the named person.

Section 6 (Restrictions on Extraordinary Payments in Connection with the International Space Station) prohibits any agency of the U.S. government from making extraordinary payments to the Russian Aviation and Space Agency, or any affiliates, or the Government of the Russian Federation, or any entities of the government, until the president determines and reports to Congress that (1) it is the Russian government's policy "to oppose the proliferation to or from Iran or Syria of weapons of mass destruction and missile systems capable of delivering such weapons;" (2) the Russian government has demonstrated a commitment to preventing transfers of such goods to or from Iran or Syria; and (3) the Russian Aviation and Space Agency, or its affiliates, has not made such transfers to or from Iran or Syria in the preceding year (other than those allowed by the president's certification for exemptions).

The president may allow extraordinary payments when "such payments are necessary to prevent the imminent loss of life by or grievous injury to individuals aboard the International Space Station." This allowance requires the president to notify to Congress such payments will be allowed, and to report to Congress on details within 30 days of the initial notification. The president may also allow extraordinary payments for specific development programs of the International Space Station provided he notify Congress ahead of payment and that the recipients of that payment are not subject to nonproliferation sanctions.

P.L. 106-178; approved March 14, 2000. Originally enacted as the Iran Nonproliferation Act of 2000. Sec. 4(e) of the Iran Nonproliferation Amendments Act of 2005 (P.L. 109-112; approved November 22, 2005) inserted the reference to Syria, and that Act broadened the application of the original Act to encompass transfers to and from both Iran and Syria. The North Korea Nonproliferation Act of 2006 (P.L. 109-353; approved October 13, 2006) inserted the reference to North Korea throughout the Act. Sec. 125 of the Continuing Appropriations Resolution, 2009 (division A of P.L. 110-329; approved September 30, 2008) amended text unrelated to sanctions authorities.

Sec. 1306 of the Foreign Relations Authorization Act, Fiscal Year 2003 (P.L. 107-228; approved September 30, 2002), added the reference to weapons listed on the Wassenaar Arrangement Munitions List. See also sec. 708 of the Security Assistance Act of 2000 (P.L. 106-280; 114 Stat. 862; 22 USC. 2797b note; approved October 6, 2000), which requires the president to certify that any Russian person he identifies as "a party to an agreement related to commercial cooperation on MTCR equipment or technology with a

United States person" is not also one who transfers goods, services, or technology to Iran, as identified pursuant to sec. 2(a)(1)(B) of this Act.

Iran Sanctions Act of 1996[34]

Section 4 (Multilateral Regime) authorizes the president to waive, on a case-by-case basis, sanctions imposed on any national of another country found to be investing in Iran's oil capabilities if he finds it vital to U.S. national security interests to do so. The section also authorizes the president to waive, on a case-by-case, basis, sanctions imposed on persons (as defined by the Act in sec. 14) whose government of jurisdiction cooperates "with the United States in multilateral efforts to prevent Iran from acquiring or developing chemical, biological, or nuclear weapons, or related technologies; or ... acquiring or developing destabilizing numbers and types of advanced conventional weapons...." The president is required to determine such a waiver is vital to U.S. national security interests and report details to Congress. The president is required to investigate any person for which "credible information" indicates that person is engaged in sanctionable activity.

Section 5 (Imposition of Sanctions) requires the president to impose sanctions on any person found to have invested in Iran's ability to develop petroleum resources, or sold, leased or provided Iran refined petroleum products or related technology, information, or support. The president is required to impose three or more of the sanctions listed in section 6 on any person he finds has, after July 1, 2010 (the date of enactment of amendments in the Comprehensive Iran Sanctions, Accountability, and Divestment Act of 2010), "exported, transferred, or otherwise provided to Iran any goods, services, technology, or other items knowing that the provision of such ... items would contribute materially to the ability of Iran to ... acquire or development chemical, biological, or nuclear weapons or related technologies; or acquire or develop destabilizing numbers and types of advanced conventional weapons." In addition, the president is required to deny export licenses to any person subject to these sanctions, and the government of primary jurisdiction for the sanctioned person is also to be denied transfer or retransfer "of any nuclear material, facilities, components, or other goods, services, or technology that are or would be subject to an agreement for cooperation between the United States and that government" unless the president determines that the government "does not know or have reason to know about the activity" or "has taken, or is taking all reasonably steps

Nuclear, Biological, Chemical, and Missile Proliferation Sanctions 105

necessary to prevent a recurrence of the activity and to penalize the person for the activity." The president also may waive the sanctions if he finds it "vital to the national security interests of the United States" to do so, and so notifies the Committees on Foreign Affairs and Foreign Relations.

Section 6 (Description of Sanctions) authorizes the president to employ a range of punitive measures, including denial of Export-Import funding, denial of export licenses, prohibition on U.S. government and commercial bank financing, refusal of U.S. government procurement contracts, prohibition on foreign exchange transactions, limit on financial transactions including credit and inter-bank payments with banks under U.S. jurisdiction, prohibition on transactions related to property under U.S. jurisdiction, and additional measures as the president sees fit.

Under language added by the Comprehensive Iran Sanctions, Accountability, and Divestment Act of 2010, persons entering into a U.S. government contract are now required to certify that they do not engage in any activity that could be subject to sanctions under this Act.

Section 8 (Termination of Sanctions) cancels the requirement for sanctions if the president determines that Iran has ceased all efforts to design, develop, manufacture, or acquire weapons of mass destruction or related delivery systems, and if Iran is removed from the list of supporters of international terrorism.

Section 9 (Duration of Sanctions; Presidential Waiver) authorizes the president to delay the imposition of sanctions for up to 90 days if consultations are entered into with a government that holds jurisdiction over the offending party. Sanctions may be further delayed another 90 days if the government of jurisdiction takes action to terminate the offending behavior and penalize the offender. Otherwise, sanctions are imposed for not less than two years or until such time that the president can certify that the offending behavior has ceased, at which juncture sanctions remain in place for at least one year. Alternatively, the president may waive the imposition of sanctions if he finds it necessary to U.S. national interests to do so.

P.L. 104-172; approved August 5, 1996. Originally enacted as the Iran and Libya Sanctions Act. The president waived its application toward Libya on April 23, 2004 (see note), and the Iran Freedom Support Act (P.L. 109-293; approved September 30, 2006) struck out the reference to Libya and made other substantive changes to focus the intent of the Act solely on Iran and that country's efforts to develop weapons of mass destruction or other military capabilities. Thus, for example, where section 5 previously required the imposition of sanctions on any person found to be contributing to Libya's pursuit of weapons of mass destruction, advanced conventional weapons, or other military resources, the amended section hones in only on Iran's development of military resources. The Iran Freedom Support Act also struck out references in section 8 to Libya's complicity in the PanAm Flight 103 explosion over Lockerbie, Scotland. Previously, the Act had been amended to lower the threshold of investment in Libya that triggered the imposition of sanctions, change reporting requirements, fine-tune definitions, and extend the authorities herein another five years, to 2006 (P.L. 107-24; approved August 3, 2001). Authorities were further extended to September 29, 2006 (P.L. 109-267; approved August 4, 2006), to December 31, 2011 (P.L. 109-293), and again to December 31, 2016 (P.L. 111-195).

The Comprehensive Iran Sanctions, Divestment, and Accountability Act of 2010 (P.L. 111-195; approved July 1, 2010) substantially reframed the original Act to intensify the focus on reducing the likelihood of Iran obtaining advanced conventional weapons, weapons of mass destruction, and the means to deliver them. Amendments therein: require close cooperation with the United States in multilateral nonproliferation efforts (sec. 4(c)(1)(B)); require the president to initiate investigations and impose more sanctions for a broader range of activities at lower transaction thresholds (sec. 4(e), sec. 5);and add restrictions on foreign exchange, banking, property, and government contracts to the list of sanction options available to the president (sec. 6).

Iraq Sanctions Act of 1990[35]

This Act reaffirmed the United States' commitment to sanctions leveled by the United Nations after Iraq invaded Kuwait in August 1990. The findings, laid out in *section 586F (Declarations Regarding Iraq's Long-Standing Violations of International Law)*, cite Iraq's violation of international law relating to chemical and biological warfare, Iraq's use of chemical weapons against Iran and its own Kurdish population, efforts to expand its chemical weapons capabilities, evidence of biological weapons development, and its efforts to establish a nuclear arsenal.

Section 586C (Trade Embargo Against Iraq) continues sanctions imposed pursuant to four executive orders issued at the outset of Iraq's invasion of Kuwait. Sanctions include foreign assistance, trade, economic restrictions, and the freezing of Iraqi assets under U.S. jurisdiction. The president may alter or terminate the sanctions issued in his executive orders only with prior 15-day notification to Congress.

Nuclear, Biological, Chemical, and Missile Proliferation Sanctions 107

Section 586D (Compliance with U.N. Sanctions Against Iraq) prohibits foreign assistance, Overseas Private Investment Corporation (OPIC) funding, and assistance or sales under the AECA to countries found to be not in compliance with United Nations Security Council sanctions against Iraq. The president may waive these sanctions if he determines and certifies to Congress that assistance is in U.S. national interest, that assistance will benefit the targeted country's needy, or such assistance will be in the form of humanitarian assistance for foreign nationals fleeing Iraq and Kuwait.

Section 586G (Sanctions Against Iraq)[36] prohibits the United States from engaging in the following activities relating to Iraq: (1) U.S. foreign military sales under the AECA; (2) commercial arms sales licensing of items on the U.S. Munitions List; (3) exports of control list goods and technology, as defined by secs. 4(b) and 5(c)(1) of the Export Administration Act; (4) issuance of licenses or other authorizations relating to nuclear equipment, materials, and technology; (5) international financial institutions support; (6) Export-Import Bank funding; (7) Commodity Credit Corporation funding; and (8) foreign assistance other than emergency medical or humanitarian funding.

Pursuant to *section 586H (Waiver Authority)*, the president may waive the application of sec. 586G sanctions if he certifies to Congress that the Government of Iraq has demonstrated improved respect for human rights, does not support international terrorists, and "is not acquiring, developing, or manufacturing (I) ballistic missiles, (ii) chemical, biological, or nuclear weapons, or (iii) components for such weapons; has forsworn the first use of such weapons; and is taking substantial and verifiable steps to destroy or otherwise dispose of any such missiles and weapons it possesses..." The president must further certify that Iraq is meeting its obligations under several international agreements. Finally, the president must certify that it is in the national interest of the United States to make such a waiver and resume any or all of these economic supports. The section also authorizes the president to waive the restrictions in response to a fundamental change in Iraq's leadership, provided the new government makes credible assurances that it meets the above criteria.

Section 586I (Denial of Licenses for Certain Exports to Countries Assisting Iraq's Rocket or Chemical, Biological, or Nuclear Weapons Capability) prohibits the export licensing of supercomputers to any government (or its officials) that the president finds to be assisting Iraq in improving its rocket technology, or chemical, biological, or nuclear weapons capability. While the section includes no waiver authority, it is triggered by the president making a determination and so its implementation rests with the executive branch.

Enacted as secs. 586-586J of the Foreign Operations, Export Financing, and Related Programs Appropriations Act, 1991 (P.L. 101-513; approved November 5, 1990). It has not been amended.

National Emergencies Act

Title II (50 USC. 1621, 1622) authorizes the president to declare, administer, and terminate national emergencies. Such a condition is required for the president to exercise his authority under the International Emergency Economic Powers Act.

P.L. 94-412; approved September 14, 1976. There have been no substantive amendments specifically affecting proliferation issues.

North Korea Threat Reduction Act of 1999

The North Korea Threat Reduction Act of 1999 prohibits the entering into effect for the United States of any international agreement or agreement for cooperation with North Korea that would result in North Korea obtaining nuclear materials. The law also prohibits U.S. issuance of export licenses for, or approval for transfer or retransfer of, a specified nuclear item. To make such items available, the president must determine and report to Congress that North Korea has met certain benchmarks on the safe use of nuclear materials, including cooperation with the IAEA on inspections, compliance with IAEA safeguard agreements, compliance with terms of the Agreed Framework it reached with the United States, implementation of terms of the Joint Declaration on Denuclearization, no accrual of enriched uranium or the means to develop that material, and no efforts to acquire or develop nuclear weapon capability. The president must also determine and certify that it is the U.S. national interest to transfer key nuclear components to North Korea.

Enacted as subtitle B of title VIII of the Admiral James W. Nance and Meg Donovan Foreign Relations Authorization Act, Fiscal Years 2000 and 2001 (H.R. 3427, enacted by reference in sec. 1000(a)(7) of P.L. 106-113; 113 Stat. 1501A-472; approved November 29, 1999). Sec. 1307 of the Foreign Relations Authorization Act, Fiscal Year 2003 (P.L. 107-228; 116 Stat. 1438) amended the Act to define more clearly what nuclear-related materials require licensing for export to North Korea by citing terms and requirements in the Atomic Energy Act of 1954 and Annex A and Annex B of the Nuclear Suppliers Group.

Nuclear Non-Proliferation Act of 1978[37]

The Nuclear Non-Proliferation Act of 1978 states U.S. policy for actively pursuing more effective international controls over the transfer and use of nuclear materials, equipment, and technology for peaceful purposes in order to prevent proliferation. The policy statement includes the establishment of common international sanctions.

The Act promotes the establishment of a framework for international cooperation for developing peaceful uses of nuclear energy, authorizes the U.S. government to license exports of nuclear fuel and reactors to countries that adhere to nuclear non-proliferation policies, provides incentives for countries to establish joint international cooperative efforts in nuclear non-proliferation, and authorizes relevant export controls.

The Act requires the Nuclear Regulatory Commission to publish regulations establishing procedures for granting, suspending, revoking or amending nuclear export licenses. The Act also requires the Department of Commerce to issue regulations relating to all export items that could be of significance for nuclear explosive purposes.

Section 304(b) (Export Licensing Procedures; 42 USC. 2155a) requires the Nuclear Regulatory Commission to publish regulations establishing the procedures for granting, suspending, revoking or amending nuclear export licenses. *Section 309 (42 USC. 2139a)* similarly requires the Department of Commerce to issue regulations relating to all export items that could be of significance for nuclear explosive purposes.

Section 402 (Additional Requirements; 42 USC. 2153a) provides that, unless otherwise stated in a cooperation agreement, no source or special nuclear material exported from the United States may be enriched after exportation unless the United States approves the enrichment. The section prohibits the export of nuclear material for the purpose of enrichment or reactor fueling if the recipient country is party to a cooperation agreement with the United States amended or concluded after 1978, unless the agreement specifically allows for such transfers. Finally, the section prohibits export of any major critical component of any uranium enrichment, nuclear fuel reprocessing, or heavy water production facility, unless a cooperation agreement specifically designates these items as exportable.

110 Dianne E. Rennack

The Nuclear Non-Proliferation Act of 1978 was enacted as P.L. 95-242; approved March 10, 1978. Secs. 304(b) and 402 have not been amended. Minor changes have been incorporated into sec. 309 (42 USC. 2139a), relating to a requirement of prior consultation and the reorganization of the Department of State.

Nuclear Proliferation Prevention Act of 1994

The Nuclear Proliferation Prevention Act of 1994 was enacted to update current law to reflect growing concerns about nuclear proliferation. *Section 821 (Imposition of Procurement Sanction on Persons Engaging in Export Activities That Contribute to Proliferation; 22 USC. 6301)*[38] requires U.S. government procurement sanctions against any U.S. person or foreign person if the president determines that person has materially, and with requisite knowledge, contributed, through export of goods or technology, to efforts to acquire unsafeguarded special nuclear material, or to use, develop, produce, stockpile, or otherwise acquire a nuclear explosive device. Terms of the sanctions are that the U.S. government may not, for 12 months, procure from or enter into procurement contracts with the sanctioned individual. Sanctions may be terminated after 12 months if the president determines and certifies to Congress that the individual has stopped whatever activities that brought on the sanctions, and that the individual will not engage in such activities in the future. Otherwise, to waive the sanctions at the end of 12 months, the president must determine and certify to Congress, 20 days in advance, that continuing the sanctions would have a serious adverse effect on vital U.S. interests. The president is not required to apply or maintain sanctions if the articles or services provided are essential to U.S. national security; if the provider is a sole source; if the articles or services are essential to national security under defense cooperative agreements; if the articles constitute essential spare parts, essential component parts, routine servicing or maintenance, or information and technology essential to U.S. production. Sanctions may also not be required if the individual relied on an advisory opinion of the State Department stating that a particular activity was not deemed to be sanctionable. In the case of a foreign person, the president is required to enter into consultation with the foreign government with primary jurisdiction over that person, and thus may delay the imposition of sanctions for up to 90 days. Sanctions may be further averted if the president determines and certifies that the foreign government has taken steps to end the foreign person's activities.

Nuclear, Biological, Chemical, and Missile Proliferation Sanctions   111

Section 823 (Role of International Financial Institutions; 22 USC. 6302) requires the Secretary of the Treasury to instruct U.S. executive directors of international financial institutions to use voice and vote to oppose promotion of the acquisition of unsafeguarded special nuclear material or the development, stockpiling, or use of nuclear explosive devices by any non-nuclear-weapon state. *Section 824 (Prohibition on Assisting Nuclear Proliferation Through the Provision of Financing; 22 USC. 6303)* prohibits financial institutions and persons involved with financial institutions from assisting nuclear proliferation through the provision of financing. The section requires that when the president determines that a U.S. person or foreign person has engaged in a prohibited activity, he shall impose the following sanctions: (1) ban on dealing in U.S. government debt instruments; (2) ban on serving as a depositary for U.S. government funds; (3) ban on pursuing, directly or indirectly, new commerce in the United States; and (4) ban on conducting business from a new location in the United States. The president is required to consult with any foreign government that serves as primary jurisdiction for any foreign person sanctioned under this section. Sanctions may be delayed for 90 days while consultation with a foreign government is underway, and may be further averted if the foreign government takes steps to stop the prohibited activity. Sanctions are in place for not less than 12 months, and are terminated then only if the president determines and certifies to Congress that the person's engagement in prohibited activity has ceased and will not resume. The president may waive the continued use of sanctions when he determines and certifies to Congress that continuing the restrictions would have a serious adverse effect on the safety and soundness of the domestic or international financial system or the domestic or international payments system. *The Nuclear Proliferation Prevention Act of 1994 was enacted as title VIII of the Foreign Relations Authorization Act, Fiscal Years 1994 and 1995 (P.L. 103-236; approved April 30, 1994). Sec. 157(b) of P.L. 104-164 (approved July 21, 1996) made changes to sec. 824, including striking out a requirement that any presidential determination pursuant to subsec. (c) be reviewed by the courts.*

Syria Accountability and Lebanese Sovereignty Restoration Act of 2003[39]

Section 5 (Penalties and Authorization) requires the president to prohibit the export to Syria of any dual-use item on the U.S. Munitions List or

Commerce Control List, prohibit the issuance of export licenses for such items, and to choose from a menu of other restrictions, to impose two or more of the following: (A) prohibit the export of most U.S. products, (B) prohibit U.S. businesses from operating in Syria, (C) limit U.S. travel of Syrian diplomats, (D) prohibit landing or flyover rights to Syrian air carriers, (E) curtail diplomatic relations between the United States and Syria, or (F) block transactions in which the Government of Syria has an interest.

For sanctions to be lifted, the president must certify to Congress that four conditions have been met, that the Government of Syria has ceased: (1) providing support for international terrorist groups and does not allow terrorist groups to maintain facilities in territory under Syrian control; (2) its occupation of Lebanon; (3) "the development and deployment of medium-and long-range surface-to-surface ballistic missiles, is not pursuing or engaged in the research, development, acquisition, production, transfer, or deployment of biological, chemical, or nuclear weapons, has provided credible assurances that such behavior will not be undertaken in the future, and has agreed to allow United Nations and other international observers to verify such actions and assurances"; and (4) support for, and facilitation of, terrorist activities in Iraq.

The president may waive any or all sanctions, however, if he finds it in the U.S. national security interest to do so and notifies Congress. *P.L. 108-175; approved December 12, 2003. No amendments have been enacted.*

End Notes

[1] For a more general discussion on the use of sanctions in foreign policy, see CRS Report 97-949, Economic Sanctions to Achieve U.S. Foreign Policy Goals: Discussion and Guide to Current Law, by Dianne E. Rennack and Robert D. Shuey. For a more general discussion on proliferation, see CRS Report RL31559, Proliferation Control Regimes: Background and Status, coordinated by Mary Beth Nikitin.

[2] The International Atomic Energy Act of 1954 and the Nuclear Non-Proliferation Act of 1978 sought to increase international participation in and adherence with the International Atomic Energy Agency and Nuclear Non-Proliferation Treaty, respectively, and, to that end, authorized the president to enter into international discussions, including the imposition of sanctions against those who abrogate or violate these international agreements.

[3] The list is arranged alphabetically, with references to the U.S. Code and Legislation on Foreign Relations where applicable. Legislative history of pertinent amendments is also given, in italics.

[4] P.L. 90-629; approved October 22, 1968; 22 USC. 2751 and following. Legislation on Foreign Relations Through 2008, vol. I-A, p. 427.

[5] See also sec. 73A of the AECA (22 USC. 2797b-1), which requires the president to notify Congress when U.S. action results in any country becoming an MTCR adherent. The

Nuclear, Biological, Chemical, and Missile Proliferation Sanctions   113

section also requires an independent assessment to be submitted to Congress by the Director of Central Intelligence covering the newly designated MTCR adherent and several proliferation issues.

[6] Two versions of the Chemical and Biological Weapons Control and Warfare Elimination Act of 1991 were enacted. Title V of the Foreign Relations Authorization Act, Fiscal Years 1992 and 1992 (P.L. 102-138; approved October 28, 1991) enacted the first. Later in the same session, title III of P.L. 102-182 (a trade act otherwise unrelated to nonproliferation issues) repealed the first version and enacted a new Chemical and Biological Weapons Control and Warfare Elimination Act of 1991. This report refers only to the second enactment—that which currently stands in law.

[7] Sec. 601(b) of the International Security Assistance and Arms Export Control Act of 1976, P.L. 94-329, states what is required under "expedited procedure." See Legislation on Foreign Relations Through 2008, vol. I-A, p. 1058.

[8] Sanctions under sec. 102 were applied to India and Pakistan after each country tested nuclear explosive devices in May 1998 (India: Presidential Determination 98-22, May 13, 1998; 63 F.R. 27665) (Pakistan: Presidential Determination 98-25, May 30, 1998; 63 F.R. 31881). Congress has enacted a series of laws after the sanctions were imposed to ease their application or authorize the president to waive their application. See the Agriculture Export Relief Act of 1998 (P.L. 105-194; approved July 14, 1998), India-Pakistan Relief Act of 1998 (title IX of P.L. 105-277; approved October 21, 1998), and the Department of Defense Appropriations Act, 2000, title IX (P.L. 106-79; approved October 25, 1999), which authorized the president to waive the nuclear test-related sanctions against the two countries permanently. The president exercised this waiver authority case-by-case several times over 1999-2001, and then finally comprehensively in Presidential Determination 01-28 of September 22, 2001 (66 F.R. 50095). On September 10, 2004, the president determined that Libya had received nuclear materials and was in violation of sec. 102, but also determined that "the application of sanctions, as required by this section, would have a serious adverse effect on vital United States interests and that I have received reliable assurances that Libya will not acquire or develop nuclear weapons or assist other nations in doing so." (Presidential Determination 2004-44, September 10, 2004; 69 F.R. 56153).The president invoked sec. 102 in response to North Korea's nuclear pursuits on December 7, 2006 (Presidential Determination 2007-7; 72 F.R. 1899). See, however, sec. 1405 of the Supplemental Appropriations Act, 2008 (P.L. 110-252; 122 Stat. 2337).

[9] Medicine and food were further exempted from the application of sanctions in most cases with the enactment of the Trade Sanctions Reform and Export Enhancement Act of 2000 Act (title IX of P.L. 106-387; approved October 28, 2000).

[10] P.L. 83-703; approved August 30, 1954; 42 USC. 2011 and following. P.L. 99-183, a joint resolution approving an Agreement for Nuclear Cooperation Between the United States and China, (approved December 16, 1985; 99 Stat. 1174), requires the president to certify that China was not violating section 129 of the Atomic Energy Act of 1954. On January 12, 1998, President Clinton made such a determination, also certifying that China had met nuclear weapons nonproliferation standards stated in section 902(a)(6)(B)(i) of P.L. 101-246 (22 USC. 2151 note; often referred to as the "Tiananmen Square sanctions"). See Presidential Determination No. 98-10 (63 F.R. 3447; January 23, 1998). Section 104 of the Henry J. Hyde United States-India Peaceful Atomic Energy Cooperation Act of 2006 (P.L. 109-401; approved December 18, 2006; 22 USC. 8003) authorizes the president to exempt a proposed U.S.-India nuclear cooperation agreement from requirements of sec. 123 a.(2) of the Atomic Energy Act of 1954 (42 USC. 2153), and to waive secs. 128 and 129 of that Act

114 Dianne E. Rennack

as each would apply to India, provided the standards stated in sec. 104(b) of that Act are met. President Bush exercised this authority in Presidential Determination 2008-26 (September 10, 2008; 73 F.R. 54287).

[11] P.L. 102-182; approved December 4, 1991; 22 USC. 5601-5606.

[12] Two versions of the Chemical and Biological Weapons Control and Warfare Elimination Act of 1991 were enacted. Title V of the Foreign Relations Authorization Act, Fiscal Years 1992 and 1992 (P.L. 102-138; approved October 28, 1991) enacted the first. Later in the same session, title III of P.L. 102-182 (a trade act otherwise unrelated to nonproliferation issues) repealed the first version and enacted a new Chemical and Biological Weapons Control and Warfare Elimination Act of 1991. This report refers only to the second enactment—that which currently stands in law.

[13] Division I of P.L. 105-277; approved October 21, 1998; 112 Stat. 2681-856; 22 USC. 6701 and following. See also 18 USC. 229 and following, where the CWC Implementation Act of 1998 establishes crime and criminal procedures related to violation of the Chemical Weapons Convention.

[14] See S.Res. 75, 105th Congress, 1st Session.

[15] P.L. 111-195; 124 Stat. 1312; approved July 1, 2010. See also the Iran Sanctions Act of 1996, which CISADA substantively amended. CISADA also amended the United Nations Participation Act of 1945 (22 USC. 287c(b)), Arms Export Control Act (22 USC. 2778(c), 2780(j)), and Trading with the Enemy Act (50 USC. App. 16(a)) as each provides terms for criminal penalties relating to sanctions violations. The Act also requires the president to impose sanctions on individuals identified as human rights violators in the course and aftermath of Iran's elections of June 12, 2009 (sec. 105; 22 USC. 8514); and requires the U.S. government not to enter into or renew any procurement contract with a person who exports technology to Iran that can be used to suppress the flow of information or free speech of Iranian people, unless the president exempts the contract based on requirements free trade agreements to which the United States is a party (sec. 106; 22 USC. 8515). He may also waive the application of sanctions required under secs. 105 and 106 if he finds it in the national interest to do so and certifies to Congress (under sec. 401).

[16] P.L. 111-117; 123 Stat. 3034 at 3312 (division F of the Consolidated Appropriations Act, 2010; approved December 16, 2009). The 2nd Session of the 111th Congress has not completed work on a State Department/foreign operations appropriations bill for Fiscal Year 2011. Section 101(7) of the Continuing Appropriations Act, 2011 (P.L. 111-242; 124 Stat. 2607; approved September 30, 2011) continues appropriations stated in P.L. 111-117 through December 3, 2010.

[17] P.L. 96-72; approved September 29, 1979; 50 USC. App. 2401 and following. Authority granted by the Export Administration Act was continued to August 20, 2001, by the Export Administration Modification and Clarification Act of 2000 (P.L. 106-508; approved November 13, 2000). Approaching another expiration, President Bush invoked authority granted his office pursuant to the International Emergency Economic Powers Act and National Emergencies Act, to issue Executive Order 13222 (August 17, 2001; 66 F.R. 44025), extending authorities of the Export Administration Act for one year. On August 14, 2002, the president issued a notice to extend the authority of that executive order another year (67 F.R. 53721). Since then, Executive Order 13222 has been extended annually in presidential notices, most recently with presidential notice of August 12, 2010 (75 F.R. 50679). Such steps have precedent: the Export Administration Act expired in September 1990, to be renewed by executive order until Congress passed reauthorizing legislation in

Nuclear, Biological, Chemical, and Missile Proliferation Sanctions   115

1993. Since 1990, the authorities of the Act have been made available by either executive order, determinations renewing those orders, or short-term legislative extensions.

[18] Many laws link the support of acts of international terrorism with WMD activities. Section 40 of the Arms Export Control Act (22 USC. 2780), for example, defines acts of international terrorism, in part, as "all activities that the Secretary [of State] determines willfully aid or abet the international proliferation of nuclear explosive devices to individuals or groups, willfully aid or abet an individual or groups in acquiring unsafeguarded special nuclear material, or willfully aid or abet the efforts of an individual or group to use, development, produce, stockpile, or otherwise acquire chemical, biological, or radiological weapons." See sec. 40 of the Arms Export Control Act and sec. 620A of the Foreign Assistance Act of 1961 (22 USC. 2371), in Legislation on Foreign Relations Through 2008, vol. I-A, pages 507, 340, respectively.

[19] The Coordinating Committee for Multilateral Export Controls (COCOM) agreed to cease to exist on March 31, 1994. Member nations agreed to retain current control lists until a successor organization is established. On December 19, 1995, the United States and 27 other countries, including NATO participants and Russia, agreed to establish a new multilateral export control arrangement. In July 1996, thirty-three countries gave final approval to the Wassenaar Arrangement for Export Controls for Conventional Arms and Dual-Use Goods and Technologies ("Wassenaar Arrangement"). On January 15, 1998, the Bureau of Export Administration (BXA—now the Bureau of Industry and Security, or BIS) of the Department of Commerce issued an interim rule to implement the Wassenaar Arrangement list of dual-use items and revisions to the Commerce Control List required by implementation of the Wassenaar Arrangement (63 F.R. 2452). BXA issued a final rule on July 23, 1999 (64 F.R. 40106), and a revision to that rule where it pertains to national security controls on July 12, 2000 (65 F.R. 43130). On December 1, 2000, participants in the Wassenaar Arrangement agreed to adopt new standards for controlling exports of electronics, computers, and telecommunications technology. A current version of the Commerce Control List may be found at 15 CFR part 774, with an overview at 15 CFR part 738. See http://www.access.gpo.gov/bis/ear/ear_data.html.

[20] P.L. 79-173; approved July 31, 1945; 12 USC. 635 and following.

[21] Section 1062 of the Duncan Hunter National Defense Authorization Act for Fiscal Year 2009 (P.L. 110-417; 50 USC. 2370 note; approved October 14, 2008), requires the Secretaries of Defense, Energy, Commerce, and State, and the Nuclear Regulatory Commission to keep the Committees on Armed Services informed with respect to "any activities undertaken ... with respect to nonproliferation programs; and any other activities undertaken ... to prevent the proliferation of nuclear, chemical, or biological weapons or the means of delivery of such weapons." It further requires the Director of National Intelligence to inform the committees "with respect to any activities of foreign nations that are significant with respect to the proliferation of nuclear, chemical, or biological weapons or the means of delivery of such weapons."

[22] P.L. 87-195; approved September 4, 1961; 22 USC. 2151 et seq. See Legislation on Foreign Relations Through 2008, vol. I-A, p. 11. See also chapter 9 in this Act, relating to "Nonproliferation and Export Control Assistance," added by sec. 301 of the Security Assistance Act of 2000 (P.L. 106-280; approved October 6, 2000), further amended by the Russian Federation Debt for Nonproliferation Act of 2002 (division B, title VIII, subtitle B, of P.L. 107-228; approved September 30, 2002), and the Security Assistance Act of 2002 (division B of P.L. 107-228; approved September 30, 2002), codified at 22 USC. 2349bb et seq. This chapter does not impose sanctions; instead it makes assistance available to

friendly countries to ultimately "enhance the nonproliferation and export control capabilities ... by providing training and equipment to detect, deter, monitor, interdict, and counter proliferation."

[23] Sec. 307(d) of this Act, however, imposes no sanctions but requires the Secretary of State to report to Congress whenever he/she determines "that programs of the International Atomic Energy Agency in Iran are inconsistent with United States nuclear nonproliferation and safety goals, will provide Iran with training or expertise relevant to the development of nuclear weapons, or are being used as a cover for the acquisition of sensitive nuclear technology." Added to sec. 307 by sec. 1342 of the Iran Nuclear Proliferation Prevention Act of 2002 (subtitle D of title XIII of P.L. 107-228; approved September 30, 2002).

[24] Previously, sec. 431 of the Foreign Relations Authorization Act, Fiscal Years 1994 and 1995 (P.L. 103-236; 108 Stat. 459) struck out the Southwest Africa People's Organization (SWAPO) and added Burma, Iraq, North Korea, and Syria to this prohibition; sec. 2101 of the Emergency Supplemental Appropriations Act for Defense, the Global War on Terror, and Tsunami Relief, 2005 (P.L. 109-13; 119 Stat. 266) removed Iraq.

[25] P.L. 109-401; approved December 18, 2006; 22 USC. 8001 et seq.

[26] P.L. 95-223; 50 USC. 1701 et seq.

[27] The "situations in which authorities may be exercised" are stated in sec. 202 (50 USC. 1701).

[28] The president currently maintains restrictions on trade and transaction with a number of states, using his IEEPA authorities, for a wide range of concerns not directly relating to WMD proliferation. In some instances, however, the targeted government may also have a history of engaging in proliferation activities and, as a result, the clear lines between issues may be blurred. Other current sanctions regimes in place pursuant to IEEPA authorities include: Somalia (U.N. requirements, piracy, armed robbery at sea, arms embargo), Iran (human rights), Burma (human rights, corruption, rule of law and democracy), Sudan (regional stability, terrorism, human rights, religious freedom, slavery), Balkans (regional stability), Zimbabwe (democracy, rule of law), Iraq (post-war protection of assets), Liberia (regional stability, arms trafficking, protection of ceasefire), Cote d'Ivoire (regional stability, human rights, protection of international peacekeeping forces), Syria (terrorism, regional stability, corruption, implication in assassination of Lebanon's prime minister), Belarus (democracy), Congo (regional stability), and Lebanon (democracy). IEEPA authorities are also used to address narcotics trafficking, terrorism, and conflict diamond trade.

[29] P.L. 109-293; approved September 30, 2006; 50 USC. 1701 note. Title III of the Act, relating to democracy promotion in Iran, is codified at 22 USC. 2151 note. See also sec. 1241—Report on U.S. Engagement with Iran (123 Stat. 2538), and sec. 1254—Sense of Congress on Imposing Sanctions with Respect to Iran (123 Stat. 2550), in the National Defense Authorization Act for fiscal Year 2010 (P.L. 111-184; approved October 28, 2009).

[30] Executive Order 12957 (March 15, 1995; 60 F.R. 14615), as amended; Executive Order 12959 (May 6, 1995; 60 F.R. 24757), as amended ; and Executive Order 13059 (August 19, 1997; 62 F.R. 44531)—all codified as notes to 50 USC. 1701.

[31] 50 USC. 1701 note.

[32] 50 USC. 1701 note. Originally enacted as the Iran Nonproliferation Act of 2000.

[33] Executive order authorizing the Secretaries of Commerce, Treasury, and State to limit or prohibit some transactions to stop the proliferation of weapons of mass destruction. Issued November 14, 1994 (59 F.R. 59099); subsequently amended. See 50 USC. 1701 notes for current text.

[34] 50 USC. 1701 note; enacted originally as the Iran and Libya Sanctions Act of 1996. On April 23, 2004, the president determined that "Libya has fulfilled the requirements of United

Nuclear, Biological, Chemical, and Missile Proliferation Sanctions 117

Nations Security Council Resolution 748, adopted March 31, 1992, and United Nations Security Council Resolution 883, adopted November 11, 1993" (Presidential Determination No. 2004-30; 69 F.R. 24907). The determination met the requirements of the law to authorize the president to terminate economic sanctions imposed on Libya under this Act. The president has subsequently revoked four executive orders relating to Libya—E.O. 12538, 12543, 12544, and 12801—in Executive Order 13357 of September 20, 2004 (69 F.R. 56665), removing most of the statutory barriers to full and normal trade relations with that country. On May 12, 2006, the president certified that Libya was no longer a supporter of acts of international terrorism, and removed that country from the sec. 6(j) list (Presidential Determination No. 2006-14; 71 F.R. 31909; June 1, 2006).

[35] 50 USC. 1701 note. Sec. 1503 of the Emergency Wartime Supplemental Appropriations Act, 2003 (P.L. 108-11; approved April 16, 2003), as amended by P.L. 108-106 (approved November 6, 2003), authorized the president to "suspend the application of any provision of the Iraq Sanctions Act of 1990: Provided, That nothing in this section shall affect the applicability of the Iran-Iraq Arms Non-Proliferation Act of 1992 (P.L. 102-484), except that such Act shall not apply to humanitarian assistance and supplies: Provided further, That the president may make inapplicable with respect to Iraq section 620A of the Foreign Assistance Act of 1961 or any other provision of law that applies to countries that have supported terrorism: Provided further, That military equipment, including equipment as defined by title XVI, section 1608(1)(A) of P.L. 102-484, shall not be exported under the authority of this section: Provided further, That section 307 of the Foreign Assistance Act of 1961 shall not apply with respect to programs of international organizations for Iraq: Provided further, that provisions of law that direct the United States Government to vote against or oppose loans or other uses of funds, including for financial or technical assistance, in international financial institutions for Iraq shall not be construed as applying to Iraq: Provided further,...That the authorities contained in this section shall expire on September 30, 2005, or on the date of enactment of a subsequent Act authorizing assistance for Iraq and that specifically amends, repeals or otherwise makes inapplicable the authorities of this section, whichever occurs first." On May 7, 2003, the president issued a memorandum to suspend the application of all the provisions, other than section 586E (which establishes penalties for violating the sanctions imposed in the wake of Iraq's invasion of Kuwait in 1990), of this Act on Iraq. Presidential Determination No. 2003-23 (68 F.R. 26459).

[36] Section 1603 of the Iran-Iraq Arms Nonproliferation Act of 2000 (P.L. 102-484; 50 USC. 1701 note; approved October 23, 1992) makes sec. 586G(a)(1) through (4) of the Iran Sanctions Act of 1990 applicable to Iran.

[37] 22 USC. 3201 and following.

[38] Formerly at 22 USC. 3201 note, all the freestanding sections of the Nuclear Proliferation Prevention Act of 1994 have been reclassified as full sections of the United States Code: within title 22, at Chapter 72—Nuclear Proliferation Prevention, and therein, Subchapter 1—Sanctions for Nuclear Proliferation, and Subchapter 2—International Atomic Energy Agency [in P.L. 103-236].

[39] 22 USC. 2151 note.

In: Proliferation Security Measures   ISBN: 978-1-62081-014-9
Editors: R. D. Cooke & E. M. Velazquez © 2012 Nova Science Publishers, Inc

Chapter 3

PROLIFERATION SECURITY INITIATIVE (PSI)[*]

Mary Beth Nikitin

SUMMARY

The Proliferation Security Initiative (PSI) was formed to increase international cooperation in interdicting shipments of weapons of mass destruction (WMD), their delivery systems, and related materials. The Initiative was announced by President Bush on May 31, 2003. PSI does not create a new legal framework but aims to use existing national authorities and international law to achieve its goals. Initially, 11 nations signed on to the "Statement of Interdiction Principles" that guides PSI cooperation. As of January 2011, 97 countries (plus the Holy See) have committed formally to the PSI principles, although the extent of participation may vary by country. PSI has no secretariat, but an Operational Experts Group (OEG), made up of 21 PSI participants, coordinates activities.

Although WMD interdiction efforts took place with international cooperation before PSI was formed, supporters argue that PSI training exercises and boarding agreements give a structure and expectation of cooperation that will improve interdiction efforts. Many observers believe that PSI's "strengthened political commitment of like-minded states" to

---

[*] This is an edited, reformatted and augmented version of a Congressional Research Service publication, CRS Report for Congress RL34327, prepared for Members and Committees of Congress, from www.crs.gov, dated January 18, 2011.

cooperate on interdiction is a successful approach to counter-proliferation policy. But some caution that it may be difficult to measure the initiative's effectiveness, guarantee even participation, or sustain the effort over time in the absence of a formal multilateral framework. Others support expanding membership and improving inter-governmental and U.S. interagency coordination as the best way to improve the program. President Obama in an April 2009 speech said that PSI should be turned into a "durable international institution." The administration's 2010 Nuclear Security Strategy said it would work to turn PSI into a "durable international effort." The 2010 Nuclear Posture Review included PSI as a key part of the policy to impede sensitive nuclear trade.

BACKGROUND

President George W. Bush unveiled the Proliferation Security Initiative (PSI) in Krakow, Poland, on May 31, 2003.[1] Deemed "foremost among President Bush's efforts to stop WMD proliferation," PSI appeared to be a new channel for interdiction cooperation outside of treaties and multilateral export control regimes.[2]

In the December 2002 National Strategy to Combat Weapons of Mass Destruction (WMD) Proliferation, the Bush administration articulated the importance of countering proliferation once it has occurred and managing the consequences of WMD use. In particular, interdiction of WMD-related goods gained more prominence. U.S. policy sought to "enhance the capabilities of our military, intelligence, technical, and law enforcement communities to prevent the movement of WMD materials, technology, and expertise to hostile states and terrorist organizations."[3]

PSI was started partially in response to legal gaps revealed in an incomplete interdiction of the *So San*, a North Korean-flagged ship that was carrying Scud missiles parts to Yemen in December 2002. It was interdicted on the high seas by a Spanish warship after a tip from American intelligence. The boarding was legal because there was no ship under that name in the North Korean registry. Inspectors found 15 complete Scud-like missiles, 15 warheads, and missile fuel oxidizer hidden on board. However, U.S. and Spanish authorities had no legal basis to seize the cargo, and the ship was released. Yemen claimed ownership of the missiles and reportedly promised the United States that it would not retransfer the items or purchase additional missiles from North Korea. While it is not clear that if this incident had occurred after PSI was formed the outcome would have been different, it was clearly an impetus to quickly bring a multilateral interdiction coordination mechanism to fruition.[4]

PARTICIPATION IN PSI

Ten nations initially joined the United States to improve cooperation to interdict shipments (on land, sea, or in the air) of WMD, their delivery systems, and related materials.[5] According to State Department officials, this core group defined the basic principles of interdiction and worked to expand support in the early years, but was later expanded to the 20 members of the Operational Experts Group (see below).

The State Department website shows that currently 97 countries (including the United States) plus the Holy See participate in the initiative (see the *Appendix*). Requirements for participation appear to be fairly weak. This language may have been in part a result of early resistance to the idea of PSI in the international community, in particular hesitancy over sovereignty and free passage issues, as well as U.S. policymakers' intention to keep the arrangement informal and nonbinding. For example, participating states are *encouraged* to [emphasis added in italics]

- formally commit to and publicly endorse, if possible, the Statement of Principles;
- review and provide information on current national legal authorities and indicate willingness to strengthen authorities as appropriate;
- identify specific national assets that might contribute to PSI efforts;
- provide points of contact for interdiction requests;
- be willing to actively participate in PSI interdiction training exercises and actual operations as they arise; and
- be willing to consider signing relevant agreements or to otherwise establish a concrete basis for cooperation with PSI efforts.[6]

Organization

PSI has no international secretariat and no distinct program funding. The participants hold regular high-level meetings and exercises to test interdiction techniques.[7] Some consider the lack of formal mechanisms as advantageous.

Others, particularly early-on, questioned the seriousness of the effort as well as its sustainability, as long as no formal mechanisms are created.[8] The current configuration does not legally bind PSI adherents to this cooperative endeavor.

An informal coordinating structure has developed through an Operational Experts Group (OEG), which discuss proliferation concerns and plans future exercises. The OEG consists of military, law enforcement, intelligence, legal, and diplomatic experts from 21 PSI states.[9] South Korea became an OEG member in November 2010.[10] The Deputy Assistant Secretary of Defense for Countering Weapons of Mass Destruction leads the U.S. delegation to PSI OEG meetings.

MEASURING SUCCESS

Since its inception, there has been little publicly available information by which to measure PSI's success. One measurement might be the number of interdictions successfully carried out as a result of PSI countries cooperating. Secretary of State Condoleeza Rice, on the second anniversary of PSI, announced that PSI was responsible for 11 interdictions in the previous nine months.[11] On June 23, 2006, Under Secretary for Arms Control and International Security Robert Joseph reported that between April 2005 and April 2006, PSI partners worked together "on roughly two dozen separate occasions to prevent transfers of equipment and materials to WMD and missile programs in countries of concern."[12] In July 2006, Under Secretary Joseph said that PSI had "played a key role in helping to interdict more than 30 shipments."[13] He also said that PSI cooperation stopped exports to Iran's missile program and the export of heavy water-related equipment to Iran's nuclear program. However, whether and to what extent PSI has contributed to these interdictions is unclear; they may have happened even without PSI.[14] Moreover, even if the creation of PSI was followed by increased numbers of WMD-related interdictions, the increase may be the product of an upsurge in proliferation activity or improved intelligence. PSI coordination may also have benefits for interdiction efforts overall, and the need to attribute an operation to PSI appears to have receded.

Another way to gauge success might be to examine the completeness of membership in PSI, particularly of countries of highest proliferation of transshipment concern. For example, some states, such as China, Malaysia, Pakistan, and South Africa, remain outside the initiative.[15] It should be noted, however, that some countries that are not ready to sign up as full participants

Proliferation Security Initiative (PSI)   123

do attend PSI exercises as observers.[16] Other countries may participate indirectly in interdictions or information exchange related to WMD proliferation without becoming a full participant in PSI. India has attended PSI exercises as an observer, but has not yet formally joined PSI, despite U.S. encouragement.[17]

An additional issue affecting successful implementation is conclusion of ship-boarding agreements, particularly with "flags of convenience" countries. So far, the United States has signed eleven ship-boarding agreements: in 2004 with Panama, the Marshall Islands, and Liberia; in 2005 with Croatia, Cyprus, and Belize; in 2007 with Malta and Mongolia; and in 2008 with the Bahamas; in 2010 with Antigua and Barbuda, and with Saint Vincent and the Grenadines. Such arrangements typically allow two hours to deny U.S. personnel the right to board a ship.

When a merchant ship registers under a foreign flag to avoid taxes, save on wages or avoid government restrictions, it is called a flag of convenience (FOC). FOCs are of particular concern for proliferation reasons because of looser government regulations over their shipments and the ease with which ships can switch from one registry to another to avoid tracking. Thirty-two countries have flags of convenience registries.[18] Of these, Antigua and Barbuda, the Bahamas, Belize, Cambodia, Cyprus, Georgia, Honduras, Liberia, Malta, Marshall Islands, Mongolia, Panama, St. Vincent, Sri Lanka and Vanuatu are PSI participants. Panama and Liberia have the highest volume of FOC global trade.[19]

OBJECTIVES AND METHODS

The FY2011 Congressional Budget Justification for the Department of State describes PSI's mission: "a commitment by over 90 states to take action to interdict shipments, disrupt proliferation networks, and shut down the front companies that support them." The long-term objective of PSI participants is to "create a web of counter-proliferation partnerships through which proliferators will have difficulty carrying out their trade in WMD and missile-related technology."[20] It functions as an "activity, not an organization" and envisions countries working in concert to bolster their national capacities to interdict WMD shipment using a "broad range of legal, diplomatic, economic, military and other tools."[21]

Several approaches under the PSI framework may help improve interdiction efforts. First, participating states agree to review their own relevant national legal authorities to ensure that they can take action. Second, participating states resolve to take action, and to "seriously consider providing consent ... to boarding and searching of its own flag vessels by other states."[22] Third, participating states seek to put in place agreements, such as ship-boarding agreements, with other states in advance, so that no time is lost should interdiction be required. A fourth aspect is participating in joint interdiction exercises.

As many describe it, PSI relies on the "broken tail-light scenario": officials look for all available options to stop suspected transport of WMD or WMD-related items. In practice, cargos can be seized in ports if they violate the host state's laws, hence the focus on strengthening domestic laws. On the high seas, ships have the rights of freedom of the seas and innocent passage under the Law of the Sea Convention and customary international law. The boarding agreements may allow for boarding, but not necessarily cargo seizure.[23] In addition, a key gap in the PSI framework is that it applies only to commercial, not government, transportation. Government vehicles (ships, planes, trucks, etc.) cannot legally be interdicted. Thus, the missile shipments picked up by a Pakistani C-130 in the summer of 2002 in North Korea, reported by the *New York Times* in November 2002, could not have been intercepted under PSI.

The October 2003 interdiction of a shipment of uranium centrifuge enrichment parts from Malaysia to Libya illustrated the need for multilateral cooperation. The Malaysian-produced equipment was transported on a German-owned ship, the *BBC China*, leaving Dubai, passing through the Suez Canal. The United States reportedly asked the German shipping company to divert the ship into the Italian port of Taranto, where it was searched. Passage through the highly regulated Suez Canal may give authorities an opportunity to delay ships and find a reason to board them. While some Bush administration officials have cited this as an example of a successful PSI interdiction, others have argued it was part of a separate operation, and thus should not be used as evidence of PSI's success.[24]

Officials have emphasized that under PSI, states will develop "new means to disrupt WMD trafficking at sea, in the air, and on land."[25] PSI exercises have been held to practice interdictions in all of these environments.[26] In his 2004 speech introducing the initiative, President Bush proposed expanding PSI to address more than shipments and transfers, including "shutting down facilities, seizing materials, and freezing assets."[27] However, dual-use nature of some of the goods complicates these actions. In addition, while it may be comparatively easier to target shipments to states, such as Iran or North

Korea, targeting terrorist acquisitions may be a greater challenge for intelligence agencies.

Another focus for PSI has been the targeting of proliferation finance. On June 23, 2006, 66 PSI states participated in a High Level Political Meeting in Poland, which focused on developing closer ties with the business community to further prevent any financial support to the proliferation of WMD.[28] PSI states have also hosted at least four workshops to introduce industry representatives to PSI goals and principles.[29]

LEGAL AUTHORITIES

U.S. officials have been careful to emphasize that PSI actions, including ship boarding and seizures, would be carried out in accordance with national legal authorities and international law and frameworks. The Statement of Interdiction Principles commits participants to "review and work to strengthen their relevant national legal authorities where necessary to accomplish these objectives, and work to strengthen when necessary relevant international law and frameworks in appropriate ways to support these commitments." There are differing opinions on whether the United States should work more aggressively to expand international legal authority for interdictions on the high seas and in international airspace. The 2005 Protocol to the Convention for the Suppression of Unlawful Acts Against the Safety of Maritime Navigation (SUA) would require states to criminalize transportation of WMD materials and their delivery vehicles. This protocol also "creates a ship boarding regime based on flag state consent similar to agreements that the United States has concluded bilaterally as part of the Proliferation Security Initiative."[30] The United States Senate gave its advice and consent for ratification of the 2005 SUA Protocol on September 25, 2008. The administration submitted appropriate implementing legislation to the Senate Judiciary Committee in March 2010. A further step could be adoption of a U.N. resolution that would provide for interdiction activities under Section VII of the U.N. Charter, which allows the Security Council to authorize sanctions or the use of force to compel states to comply with its resolutions.

The Bush administration has in the past attempted to expand international legal authority for PSI and related activities. The State Department has said that participating in PSI is a way for states to comply with their obligations under UN Security Council resolutions 1718, 1737, 1747, 1803, and 1540.[31] U.N. Security Council Resolution 1540, passed in April 2004, requires all states to establish and enforce effective domestic controls over WMD and WMD-related materials in production, use, storage, and transport; to maintain effective border controls; and to develop national export and trans-shipment controls over such items, all of which should help interdiction efforts.[32] While UNSCR 1540 was adopted under Chapter VII of the UN Charter, the resolution did not provide any enforcement authority, nor did it specifically mention interdiction or PSI. Early drafts of the resolution put forward by the United States had included explicit language calling on states to interdict if necessary shipments related to WMD. However, over China's objections, the word "interdict" was removed and was changed to "take cooperative action to prevent illicit trafficking" in WMD.[33]

UN Security Council 1874 does establish procedures for the required interdiction of WMD and other weapons going to or from North Korea. The PSI mechanism may assist countries in coordinating these actions.[34]

The Law of the Sea Convention may affect PSI implementation and is under consideration in the Senate. Secretary of State Hilary Clinton said in her confirmation hearing that ratification of the Convention is an administration priority. The Convention has also been supported by the Pentagon as a way to enhance PSI efforts. In a letter from the Joint Chiefs of Staff sent to the Senate in 2007, the Joint Chiefs argued for ratification, explaining that the convention "codifies navigation and overflight rights and high seas freedoms that are essential for the global mobility of our armed forces."[35] The letter said that the Convention supports the efforts of the Proliferation Security Initiative. Senior military officials have also publicly said that not being a party hinders efforts to recruit new PSI participants.[36] In his testimony before a Senate Armed Services Committee in April 2008, Vice Chief of Naval Operations Admiral Patrick Walsh said, "Our current non-party status constrains our efforts to develop enduring maritime partnerships. It inhibits us in our efforts to expand the Proliferation Security Initiative."[37]

ISSUES FOR CONGRESS

It may remain difficult for Congress to track PSI's success. However, reporting and coordination requirements now in public law may result in more information than was available in the past. The Implementing Recommendations of the 9/11 Commission Act of 2007 (P.L. 110-53) requires the president to include PSI activities for each involved Agency in his budget request, and requires submission to Congress of joint DOD-DOS reports to include detailed three-year plans for PSI activities no later than the first Monday in February each year.[38] The Act also

recommends that PSI be expanded, that the United States should use the intelligence and planning resources of the NATO alliance, make participation open to non-NATO countries, and encourage Russia and China to participate.[39] It gives the sense of Congress that PSI should be strengthened and expanded by establishing a clear authority for PSI coordination and increasing PSI cooperation with all countries.

While PSI generally receives bipartisan support in principle, critics urge changes, such as increased transparency, expansion of participants, and improved coordination, rather than an end to the program. For example, the 9/11 Commission recommended that the United States seek to strengthen and expand PSI's membership.[40] Others emphasize coordination. Senator Richard Lugar has said, "PSI is an excellent step forward, but what is lacking is a coordinated effort to improve the capabilities of our foreign partners so that they can play a larger detection and interdiction role."[41]

U.S. government organization and management issues have also been highlighted as areas for improvement. The General Accounting Office published a report in September 2006, "Better Controls Needed to Plan and Manage Proliferation Security Initiative Activities," that recommended the following: (1) the Departments of Defense and State establish clear roles and responsibilities, interagency communication mechanisms, documentation requirements, and indicators to measure program results; (2) the Departments of Defense and State develop a strategy to work with PSI-participating countries to resolve issues that are impediments to interdictions; and (3) a multilateral mechanism be established to increase coordination, cooperation, and compliance among PSI participants.[42]

These recommendations were also endorsed by Congress in P.L. 110-53, the Implementing Recommendations of the 9/11 Commission Act of 2007. The president was required to submit a report to Congress on implementation of these recommendations, which was done past the mandated deadline, in July 2008.

A follow-up GAO report issued in November 2008 details U.S. agencies' efforts to increase PSI cooperation and coordination.[43] It reported that the Bush administration had not issued a directive to U.S. agencies to coordinate PSI functions, as required by law. A joint report by the Department of Defense and the State Department was submitted to Congress in January 2009. The Obama administration has said that it would like to "institutionalize PSI" as part of its agenda.[44] This could include following the mandates in the 9/11 Commission Act of 2007, although details have not yet been announced.

Geographic expansion of PSI participants remains a key issue—particularly how to engage China and India, as well as states in important regions like the Arabian Peninsula.[45] Congress may also consider how intelligence resources are handled.

Is intelligence sufficient and are there intelligence-sharing requirements with non-NATO allies? Also, how is PSI coordinated with other federal interdiction-related programs (e.g., export control assistance, WMD detection technologies, etc.)?

One potential complication for congressional oversight of PSI is the absence of a way to measure PSI's success, relative to past efforts. Congress may choose to consider, again, how successfully the recommendations of P.L. 110-53 have been followed, and whether more non-proliferation policy coordination within the U.S. government may be required.

Related Treaties and Conventions

On October 1, 2007, the Senate Committee on Foreign Relations received the Protocol of 2005 to the Convention for the Suppression of Unlawful Acts against the Safety of Maritime Navigation (the "2005 SUA Protocol") for consideration.[46]

The protocol was signed by the United States on February 17, 2006. In President Bush's submission note to the Senate, he summarizes the importance of this protocol to PSI activities: "The 2005 SUA Protocol also provides for a ship-boarding regime based on flag state consent that will provide an international legal basis for interdiction at sea of weapons of mass destruction, their delivery systems and related materials."

On July 29, 2008, the committee unanimously ordered the resolutions to advise and consent to the 2005 SUA Protocol. The full Senate approved the Protocol on September 25, 2008. The Senate must next approve implementing legislation for ratification to be finalized.

As mentioned above, the Senate is considering consent to ratification of the Law of the Sea Convention which military and other government officials argue will positively impact PSI implementation. Critics of the Treaty cite concerns about limiting U.S. sovereignty. The Senate Foreign Relations Committee recommended advice and consent for U.S. adherence to the treaty on October 31, 2007.

Legislation in the 111th Congress

In the 111th Congress, legislation was introduced in support of PSI. H.Res. 604, introduced by House Foreign Affairs Committee Ranking Member Ileana Ros-Lehtinen, recognizes "the vital role of the Proliferation Security Initiative in preventing the spread of weapons of mass destruction." Representative Ros-Lehtinen's proposed bill, the Western Hemisphere Counterterrorism and Nonproliferation Act of 2009 (H.R. 375) includes a sense of Congress that PSI has "repeatedly demonstrated its effectiveness in preventing the proliferation of weapons of mass destruction," and that the Secretary of State should seek to secure the "formal or informal cooperation by Western Hemisphere countries" for PSI.

The Foreign Relations Authorization Act for Fiscal Years 2010 and 2011 (H.R. 2410) called for "the expansion and greater development of the Proliferation Security Initiative (PSI)". The associated H.Rept. 111-136, in its section on minority views praises PSI thus: "The Proliferation Security Initiative is an outstanding example of U.S. leadership in the area of nonproliferation. The PSI has demonstrated that success can be achieved through a flexible consensus of like-minded countries without the need for an international bureaucracy, constraining treaties, or formal permission that often never comes."

The Comprehensive Iran Sanctions, Accountability, and Divestment Act of 2010 (P.L. 111-195) calls for any countries designated as destinations of diversion concern to be encouraged to participate in PSI and to conclude a ship-boarding agreement with the United States.

APPENDIX. PSI PARTICIPANTS (AS OF 1/01/11)

1.	Afghanistan	50.	Latvia
2.	Albania	51.	Liberia
3.	Andorra	52.	Libya
4.	Angola	53.	Liechtenstein
5.	Antigua and Barbuda	54.	Lithuania
6.	Argentina*	55.	Luxembourg
7.	Armenia	56.	Macedonia
8.	Australia*	57.	Malta
9.	Austria	58.	Marshall Islands

Appendix. (Continued)

10.	Azerbaijan	59.	Moldova
11.	The Bahamas	60.	Mongolia
12.	Bahrain	61.	Montenegro
13.	Belarus	62.	Morocco
14.	Belgium	63.	The Netherlands*
15.	Belize	64.	New Zealand*
16.	Bosnia	65.	Norway*
17.	Brunei Darussalam	66.	Oman
18.	Bulgaria	67.	Panama
19.	Cambodia	68.	Papua New Guinea
20.	Canada*	69.	Paraguay
21.	Chile	70.	Philippines
22.	Colombia	71.	Poland*
23.	Croatia	72.	Portugal*
24.	Cyprus	73.	Qatar
25.	Czech Republic	74.	Romania
26.	Denmark*	75.	Russia*
27.	Djibouti	76.	Samoa
28.	El Salvador	77.	Saudi Arabia
29.	Estonia	78.	San Marino
30.	Fiji	79.	Serbia
31.	Finland	80.	Singapore*
32.	France*	81.	Slovakia
33.	Georgia	82.	Slovenia
34.	Germany*	83.	Spain*
35.	Greece*	84.	Sri Lanka
36.	Holy See	85.	St. Vincent and the Grenadines
37.	Honduras	86.	Sweden
38.	Hungary	87.	Switzerland
39.	Iceland	88.	Tajikistan
40.	Iraq	89.	Tunisia
41.	Ireland	90.	Turkey*
42.	Israel	91.	Turkmenistan
43.	Italy*	92.	Ukraine

Proliferation Security Initiative (PSI)   131

44.	Japan*	93.	United Arab Emirates
45.	Jordan	94.	United Kingdom*
46.	Kazakhstan	95.	United States*
47.	Republic of Korea*	96.	Uzbekistan
48.	Kyrgyzstan	97.	Vanuatu
49.	Kuwait	98.	Yemen

Source: State Department website, http://www.state.
Note: * Member of Operational Experts Group.

End Notes

[1] Remarks by the President to the People of Poland, May 31, 2003. http://georgewbush-whitehouse.archives.gov/news/ releases/2003/05/20030531-3.html

[2] John R. Bolton, former Under Secretary for Arms Control and International Security, Testimony Before the House International Relations Committee, "The Bush administration's Nonproliferation Policy: Successes and Future Challenges," March 30, 2004. See also CRS Report RL31559, Proliferation Control Regimes: Background and Status, coordinated by Mary Beth Nikitin.

[3] White House, National Strategy to Combat Weapons of Mass Destruction (WMD), December 2002, p. 2.

[4] Jofi Joseph, "The Proliferation Security Initiative: Can Interdiction Stop Proliferation?" Arms Control Today, June 2004, at http://www.armscontrol.org/act/2004_06/Joseph.asp; Andrew C. Winner, "The Proliferation Security Initative: The New Face of Interdiction," The Washington Quarterly, Spring 2005, at http://www.twq.com/05spring/docs/ 05spring_winner.pdf.

[5] Australia, France, Germany, Italy, Japan, the Netherlands, Poland, Portugal, Spain, and the United Kingdom.

[6] U.S. Department of State, Fact Sheet, "Proliferation Security Initiative Frequently Asked Questions (FAQ)," May 26, 2005, available at http://www.state.gov/t/np/rls/fs/46839.htm.

[7] See http://www.state.gov/t/isn/c27700.htm for a calendar of PSI activities.

[8] See transcript from Senate Government Affairs Committee, Subcommittee on Budget and International Security, hearing on WMD and counterproliferation, June 23, 2004.

[9] The 21 members of the OEG are: Argentina, Australia, Canada, Denmark, France, Germany, Greece, Italy, Japan, the Netherlands, New Zealand, Norway, Poland, Portugal, Republic of Korea, Russia, Singapore, Spain, Turkey, United Kingdom and the United States. http://www.state.gov/t/isn/115491.htm

[10] "S. Korea Joins Leadership of U.S.-led Campaign Against Spread of WMD," Yonhap, November 1, 2010.

[11] See http://www.state.gov/secretary/rm/2005/46951.htm for the text of Secretary Rice's speech.

[12] Under Secretary for Arms Control and International Security Robert Joseph, Warsaw, Poland, June 23, 2006. Available at http://www.state.gov/t/us/rm/68269.htm.

[13] Under Secretary for Arms Control and International Security Robert Joseph, Remarks to the Capitol Hill Club, July 18, 2006, at http://www.state.gov/t/us/rm/69124.htm.

[14] Before PSI was announced, the U.S. was already cooperating with other countries to interdict WMD shipments.

[15] U.S. General Accounting Office, "U.S. Efforts to Combat Nuclear Networks Need Better Data on Proliferation Risks and Program Results," GAO-08-21, October 2007, at http://www.gao.gov/new.items/d0821.pdf.

[16] For example, India and Malaysia were observers at the October 13-15, 2007, "Pacific Shield 07" exercise off the coast of Japan. Stephanie Lieggi, "Proliferation Security Initiative Exercise Hosted by Japan Shows Growing Interest in Asia But No Sea Change in Key Outsider States," WMD Insights, December 2007-January 2008 Issue.

[17] Stephanie Lieggi, "Proliferation Security Initiative Exercise Hosted by Japan Shows Growing Interest in Asia But No Sea Change in Key Outsider States," WMD Insights, December 2007-January 2008 Issue; Valencia, Mark J., "The Proliferation Security Initiative: Making Waves in Asia," The International Institute for Security Studies, October 2005, p. 66.

[18] As designated by the International Transportation Workers' Federation, the following are flag of convenience states: Antigua and Barbuda, Bahamas, Barbados, Belize, Bermuda (UK), Bolivia, Burma, Cambodia, Cayman Islands, Comoros, Cyprus, Equatorial Guinea, French International Ship Register (FIS), German International Ship Register (GIS), Georgia, Gibraltar (UK), Honduras, Jamaica, Lebanon, Liberia, Malta, Marshall Islands (USA), Mauritius, Mongolia, Netherlands Antilles, North Korea, Panama, Sao Tome and Principe, St. Vincent, Sri Lanka, Tonga, and Vanuatu. See http://www.itfglobal.org/flags-conve nience/flags-convenien-183.cfm.

[19] Review of Maritime Transport 2009, United Nations Conference on Trade and Development, http://www.unctad.org/ en/docs/rmt2009_en.pdf

[20] John Bolton, Testimony to the House International Relations Committee, March 30, 2004.

[21] "Proliferation Security Initiative Frequently Asked Questions," U.S. State Department Bureau of Nonproliferation Fact Sheet, January 11, 2005, at http://www.state.gov /t/isn/rls/ fs/ 32725.htm.

[22] See September 2003 Statement of Interdiction Principles.

[23] See CRS Report RL32097, Weapons of Mass Destruction Counterproliferation: Legal Issues for Ships and Aircraft, by Jennifer K. Elsea.

[24] Assistant Secretary of State John Wolf told Arms Control Today that the BBC China was a "separate" operation from PSI. The interdiction was reportedly part of an intelligence operation against the A.Q. Khan network and was timed to spur Libyan disarmament. See Wade Boese, "Key U.S. Interdiction Initiative Claim Misrepresented," http://www. Armscontrol.org/act/2005_07-08/Interdiction_Misrepresented.asp; Ron Suskind, The One Percent Doctrine, 2006, pp. 268-269.

[25] Ibid.

[26] See list of all activities at http://www.state.gov/t/isn/c27700.htm

[27] See http://www.whitehouse.gov/response/index.html for text of president's speech.

[28] See "Cracow Proliferation Security Initiative High Level Political Meeting," Summary from the Polish government, at http://www.psi.msz.gov.pl/index.php?&PHPSESSID =50078a65 ad2acf1dd3d7f518b7148e58.

[29] U.S. General Accounting Office, "U.S. Efforts to Combat Nuclear Networks Need Better Data on Proliferation Risks and Program Results," GAO-08-21, October 2007, at http://www. gao.gov/new.items/d0821.pdf.

[30] Treaty Document 110-8. See http://frwebgate.access.gpo.gov/cgi-bin/getdoc.cgi? dbname= 110_cong_documents& docid=f:td008.110.pdf.

Proliferation Security Initiative (PSI) 133

[31] "Proliferation Security Initiative Frequently Asked Questions," State Department Fact Sheet, May 22, 2008.

[32] The U.N. Security Council extended the mandate of the committee in 2006 with Resolution 1673, and in 2008 with Resolution 1810. See UN 1540 Committee website, http://www. un.org/sc/1540/index.shtml.

[33] For a history of the 1540 Resolution's evolution, see Merav Datan, "Security Council Resolution 1540: WMD and Non-State Trafficking," Disarmament Diplomacy, Issue No. 79, April/May 2005, at http://www.acronym.org.uk/dd/ dd79/79md.htm.

[34] See CRS Report R40684, North Korea's Second Nuclear Test: Implications of U.N. Security Council Resolution 1874, coordinated by Mary Beth Nikitin and Mark E. Manyin.

[35] "Military Officials Urge Accession to Law of the Sea Treaty," Armed Forces Press Service, December 10, 2007.

[36] Capt. Patrick J. Neher, Judge Advocate General's Corps, Letter to the Editor, The Washington Times, November 14, 2007, at http://www.washingtontimes.com/apps/pbcs.dll/ article? AID=/20071114/EDITORIAL/111140015&template= nextpage; "Military, Civilian Officials Urge Accession to Law of Sea Treaty,"American Forces Press Service, September 28, 2007, at http://www.militaryconnection.com/news/september-2007/law-sea-treaty.html.

[37] http://armed-services.senate.gov/statemnt/2008/April/Walsh%2004-01-08.pdf

[38] Sections 1821 and 1822, The Implementing Recommendations of the 9/11 Commission Act of 2007, P.L. 110-53.

[39] Note that Russia joined PSI as a full participant in May 2004.

[40] Report of the 9/11 Commission, p. 381.

[41] Richard Lugar, "Revving Up the Cooperative Nonproliferation Regime," The Nonproliferation Review, July 2008 http://cns.miis.edu/npr/pdfs/152_viewpoint_lugar.pdf

[42] GAO-06-937C, as summarized in P.L. 110-53.

[43] GAO-09-43, "U.S. Agencies Have Taken Some Steps, but More Effort Is Needed to Strengthen and Expand the Proliferation Security Initiative," November 2008.

[44] http://www.whitehouse.gov/agenda/homeland_security/

[45] "The Proliferation Security Initiative: Three Years On," British American Security Information Council, August 2, 2006. See http://www.basicint.org/pubs/Note s/BN060802. pdf#search= %222%20august%20psi%20basic%20notes%22.

[46] Treaty Document 110-8. See http://frwebgate.access.gpo.gov/cgi-bin/getdoc.cgi?dbname= 110_cong_documents& docid=f:td008.110.pdf.

INDEX

A

access, 3, 4, 5, 14, 17, 24, 25, 27, 36, 41, 54, 80, 85, 115, 132, 133
acquisitions, 125
administrative support, 38
affirming, 45, 47
age, vii, 1, 10
agencies, vii, viii, 1, 6, 7, 9, 10, 28, 29, 63, 125, 127
aggression, 54
agriculture, 75
air carriers, 112
assassination, 116
assessment, 40, 44, 61, 113
assets, 81, 82, 99, 100, 106, 116, 121, 124
authorities, viii, 9, 22, 79, 83, 98, 103, 106, 114, 116, 117, 119, 120, 121, 124, 125
authority, viii, 23, 27, 29, 33, 41, 49, 50, 58, 64, 65, 68, 69, 70, 73, 76, 77, 79, 82, 85, 95, 97, 98, 99, 100, 101, 107, 108, 113, 114, 117, 125, 127
awareness, 3

B

ballistic missiles, 47, 52, 55, 84, 96, 107, 112
ban, 17, 94, 111
banking, 106
banks, 105
barriers, 117

benchmarks, 108
benefits, viii, 2, 8, 14, 54, 122
black market, viii, 2, 4, 10, 17
blueprint, 15
board members, 24
bureaucracy, 129
businesses, 112

C

ceasefire, 116
certification, 34, 72, 74, 75, 76, 79, 80, 83, 103
challenges, vii, 2, 10, 14, 20, 26
children, 84
citizens, 35
civil action, 68, 69, 70
commerce, 9, 16, 24, 52, 67, 111
commercial, 29, 31, 53, 67, 82, 87, 97, 103, 105, 107, 124
commodity, 95
communication, 127
communist countries, 92
communities, 65, 120
community, 2, 4, 27, 29, 53, 121, 125
compliance, viii, 2, 9, 10, 16, 39, 40, 46, 49, 54, 64, 72, 77, 92, 93, 107, 108, 127
configuration, 122
conflict, 54, 116
conformity, 66
consensus, 3, 18, 39, 46, 129
consent, 17, 24, 124, 125, 128

construction, 25, 43, 60, 79
controversial, 19, 48
convention, 16, 17, 37, 39, 40, 126
coordination, 3, 20, 23, 28, 121, 122, 126, 127, 128
coproduction, 86, 101
corruption, 116
cost, 60
counterterrorism, 20
country of origin, 102
covering, 30, 39, 113
credentials, 3
criticism, 5
currency, 97

D

danger, 3, 40
data collection, 40
database, 99
democracy, 116
denial, 9, 33, 39, 50, 53, 70, 102, 105
deployments, 55
deposits, 17
destruction, vii, 1, 2, 20, 37, 43, 44, 46, 67, 81, 97, 100, 106, 129
detection, 22, 29, 127, 128
deterrence, 29
detonation, 30
diffusion, 4, 45
diplomacy, 9, 28, 52
directors, 34, 111
disaster, 91, 93
disaster assistance, 91
disclosure, 65, 81
diseases, 85
dismantlement, 20, 34
disposition, 16, 20, 98, 99
domestic laws, vii, 1, 10, 37, 124
donor countries, 20
donors, 20, 23
draft, 37, 48
drug trafficking, 53
dual-use items, 26, 102, 115

E

economic assistance, 82
education, 82, 91
eligibility criteria, 27
embargo, 116
embassy, 38, 48
emergency, 81, 97, 107
employment, 20
encouragement, 123
encryption, 97
end-users, 83
energy, 9, 15, 16, 23, 29, 36, 58, 78, 79, 84, 90, 109
enforcement, 2, 3, 11, 15, 22, 23, 26, 27, 42, 49, 61, 71, 89, 97, 126
environment, 19, 49, 89, 124
equipment, 4, 5, 9, 16, 26, 27, 30, 31, 34, 35, 38, 45, 46, 48, 49, 50, 51, 53, 70, 72, 74, 75, 77, 78, 79, 84, 85, 86, 87, 92, 94, 96, 103, 107, 109, 116, 117, 122, 124
evidence, 35, 49, 106, 124
evolution, 133
exercise, 26, 46, 76, 97, 108, 132
expenditures, 84
expertise, 28, 34, 35, 85, 116, 120
explosives, 26

F

faith, 16
flexibility, 64
food, 32, 41, 75, 80, 95, 113
force, 2, 18, 19, 23, 24, 30, 37, 40, 47, 64, 84, 96, 125
fraud, 70
free trade, 114
freezing, 106, 124

G

goods and services, 74, 88
guidance, 21, 47

Index

137

guidelines, 2, 26, 27, 38, 45, 46, 47, 48, 50, 52, 53, 54, 55, 59, 61, 64, 67, 69, 71, 92, 93, 96, 102

H

health, 23
hemisphere, 19
history, 10, 76, 112, 116, 133
host, 124
housing, 91

I

imbalances, 54
imports, 33, 41, 50, 73, 80, 82, 89
imprisonment, 66, 68, 69, 70
individuals, 31, 34, 47, 49, 50, 52, 69, 71, 103, 114, 115
industry, 47, 125
information exchange, 48, 123
infrastructure, 36
inspections, 16, 23, 24, 40, 108
inspectors, 24
institutions, 34, 93, 111
integration, 42
interagency coordination, ix, 120
intermediaries, 83
internally displaced, 85
intervention, 55
issues, 5, 10, 29, 35, 40, 55, 65, 70, 80, 84, 108, 113, 114, 116, 121, 127

J

jurisdiction, 72, 82, 98, 102, 104, 105, 106, 110
justification, 11, 37, 89

L

lead, 8, 18, 69
leadership, vii, 1, 10, 30, 69, 107, 129

learning, 16
legislation, vii, 1, 9, 10, 12, 17, 24, 60, 64, 65, 84, 92, 93,.114, 125, 128, 129
light, 124
loans, 31, 32, 33, 41, 67, 75, 80, 117

M

malaria, 84
man, 93
management, 127
manufacturing, 53, 107
mass, vii, 1, 46, 64, 67, 97, 100, 106, 129
materials, viii, 2, 9, 15, 16, 17, 20, 22, 23, 24, 26, 29, 30, 31, 33, 34, 35, 53, 59, 64, 71, 74, 78, 79, 81, 83, 98, 107, 108, 109, 113, 119, 120, 121, 122, 124, 125, 126, 128
measurement, 122
medical, 74, 75, 77, 88, 107
medicine, 77
membership, ix, 3, 4, 5, 10, 14, 39, 45, 47, 59, 120, 122, 127
missile defenses, 8, 55
models, 19
monopoly, 45
moratorium, 17, 25

N

narcotics, 91, 94, 116
needy, 107
negative consequences, 44
negotiating, 15

O

obstacles, 27
offenders, 16
officials, 22, 27, 48, 50, 107, 121, 124, 125, 126, 128
oil, 104
operations, 3, 33, 73, 84, 88, 94, 95, 114, 121

Index

oppression, 39
oversight, 9, 29, 36, 45, 128
ownership, 14, 120

P

participants, ix, 22, 115, 119, 121, 122, 123, 125, 126, 127, 128
peace, 23, 48, 54, 67, 91, 92, 94, 97, 98, 116
penalties, 30, 33, 35, 41, 42, 65, 66, 68, 69, 99, 102, 114, 117
permission, 30, 129
petroleum, 85, 98, 100, 104
piracy, 116
plutonium, 3, 14, 25, 30, 36
poison, 66
political leaders, 53
political power, 65
population, 106
Portugal, 56, 130, 131
precedent, 114
preparation, 41, 80
preparedness, 35
prevention, 9, 28, 84
principles, viii, 21, 22, 47, 119, 121, 125
procurement, 26, 41, 88, 101, 102, 110, 114
producers, 45
production technology, 5, 52
project, 74, 88, 92
prosperity, 23
protection, 15, 16, 17, 116
public health, 79
punishment, 16

R

radiation, 66
ratification, 17, 19, 24, 37, 92, 93, 125, 126, 128
recommendations, 91, 127, 128
recurrence, 105
refugees, 85
registries, 123

regulations, 3, 48, 49, 67, 83, 86, 98, 99, 109, 123
rejection, 5
relief, 85
reprocessing, 9, 14, 18, 25, 26, 27, 30, 31, 32, 75, 79, 109
requirements, 16, 33, 34, 41, 43, 50, 66, 68, 72, 78, 81, 83, 86, 93, 95, 96, 99, 106, 109, 113, 114, 116, 126, 127, 128
research facilities, 35, 85
resistance, 3, 121
resolution, 23, 25, 69, 74, 75, 76, 79, 84, 113, 125, 126
resources, 43, 44, 66, 85, 100, 104, 106, 127, 128
response, 8, 25, 33, 38, 94, 107, 113, 120, 132
restitution, 80
restrictions, viii, 2, 5, 8, 9, 10, 27, 30, 32, 39, 53, 79, 82, 86, 87, 95, 99, 106, 107, 111, 112, 116, 123
retaliation, 8
rights, iv, 19, 81, 112, 116, 124, 126
rule of law, 93, 116
rules, 17, 67

S

sabotage, 17
safe haven, 22
safety, 20, 79, 92, 93, 111, 116
sanctions, viii, 8, 9, 11, 12, 13, 31, 33, 34, 35, 40, 41, 50, 51, 52, 54, 55, 63, 64, 65, 70, 71, 72, 73, 74, 75, 76, 79, 80, 81, 82, 83, 85, 86, 87, 88, 90, 94, 95, 99, 100, 101, 102, 103, 104, 105, 106, 107, 109, 110, 112, 113, 114, 115, 116, 117, 125
school, 93
scope, 17, 21, 27, 30, 31, 59, 92, 93
security, viii, 4, 8, 16, 17, 18, 19, 21, 22, 25, 26, 32, 48, 54, 55, 59, 63, 67, 71, 74, 75, 76, 79, 88, 91, 96, 97, 104, 110, 133
seizure, 124
services, 32, 33, 67, 71, 77, 81, 83, 86, 89, 102, 104, 110, 133

Index 139

shape, 9, 65
slavery, 116
smuggling, 15
sovereignty, 19, 121, 128
specialists, 54
speculation, 65
speech, ix, 22, 114, 120, 124, 131, 132
stability, 32, 65, 86, 98, 116
statutes, 40, 65, 81
statutory authority, 3
stockpiling, 2, 19, 37, 81, 111
storage, 17, 23, 34, 94, 126
stress, 22
structure, ix, 24, 27, 39, 119, 122
submarines, 20, 86
supplier, 3, 26, 30, 31, 37, 47, 53, 71
suppliers, 26, 27, 52
survival, 85
sustainability, 122

T

target, 73, 124
taxes, 123
teams, 49
techniques, 121
technologies, 3, 9, 27, 30, 36, 47, 55, 83
telecommunications, 115
tensions, 25, 55
tenure, 20
territorial, 19
territory, 8, 54, 112
testing, 17, 19, 48
threats, 10, 20
toxin, 66
trade, vii, ix, 1, 5, 16, 26, 27, 39, 50, 54, 64, 68, 71, 80, 82, 100, 106, 113, 114, 116, 117, 120, 123
training, ix, 22, 35, 82, 85, 91, 116, 119, 121
transactions, 68, 73, 81, 82, 87, 90, 93, 97, 98, 100, 101, 105, 112, 116

transformation, 46
transparency, 24, 45, 127
transport, 17, 23, 124, 126
transportation, 17, 124, 125
transshipment, 122
treaties, vii, 1, 3, 4, 5, 10, 15, 18, 22, 31, 37, 38, 64, 67, 68, 120, 129
treatment, 84
triggers, viii, 64, 65
tuberculosis, 84

U

universality, 38
uranium, 3, 14, 17, 25, 30, 98, 100, 108, 109, 124

V

variations, 67
vector, 66
vehicles, 45, 46, 47, 124, 125
vessels, 124
victims, 85
violence, 98
vote, 34, 111, 117

W

wages, 123
waiver, 33, 72, 74, 76, 77, 79, 80, 82, 88, 93, 97, 101, 104, 107, 113
war, 14, 58, 64, 116
water, 26, 84, 109, 122
web, 123
withdrawal, 25, 59, 64
working groups, 29
worldwide, 21, 29
wrongdoing, 70